The Principle of Spiritual Economy

The Principle of Spiritual Economy

In Connection With Questions of Reincarnation
An Aspect of the Spiritual Guidance of Man

Rudolf Steiner

Translated and Introduced by Peter Mollenhauer

The eleven lectures presented here were given between
January and May of 1909. In the Collected edition of
Rudolf Steiner's works, the German text is called *Das
Prinzip der spirituellen Ökonomie im Zusammenhang mit
Wiederverkörperungsfragen* (GA 109).

Library of Congress Cataloging-in-Publication Data

Steiner, Rudolf, 1861–1925.
  The principle of spiritual economy in connection with
questions of reincarnation.

  Translation of: Das Prinzip der spirituellen Ökonomie
im Zusammenhang mit Wiederverkörperungsfragen.
  Eleven lectures given between Jan. and May 1909.
  Bibliography: p.
  1. Anthroposophy.   2. Reincarnation.   3. Spiritual
life.   I. Title.
BP595.S894P7513   1986   299'935   86-7915
ISBN 0-88010-163-6
        0-88010-162-8 (pbk.)

About the Publication of
Rudolf Steiner's Lectures

The works written and published by Rudolf Steiner (1861–1925) constitute the foundation of anthroposophically oriented spiritual science. From 1900 to 1924, however, Steiner also gave a number of lectures and courses to the general public and to members of the Theosophical (later the Anthroposophical) Society. At first, he himself expressed the wish not to have his lectures, which were always delivered in loose form from a few sketches, committed to paper since they were "oral communications and not intended for publication." However, after some of his listeners had increasingly prepared and circulated incomplete and erroneous written reports of these lectures, Steiner felt compelled to regulate these practices and entrusted Marie Steiner-von Sievers with the task. She had to choose stenographers, administer the reports and take care of the editing for publication. Since Rudolf Steiner did not, except in a few isolated cases, have the time to correct the reports himself, his caveat regarding all publications of lectures must be taken into consideration: "What will have to be accepted, however, is that the transcriptions not checked by me may contain some errors."

In his autobiography, *The Course of My Life* (Chapter 35), Rudolf Steiner comments on the relationship of lectures for members, which initially were available only as internal printings of manuscripts, to his public writings. The exact text of these remarks can be found at the end of this volume.

What is stated there is also applicable to the courses on special subject matters which addressed themselves to a limited circle of participants who were familiar with the foundations of spiritual science.

After the death of Marie Steiner (1867–1948), the publication of a complete edition of Rudolf Steiner's works was begun in accordance with her instructions. This volume is part of the complete edition. To the extent necessary, more information on the original texts is provided at the beginning of the "Footnotes."

Contents

Page

Introduction by Peter Mollenhauer ix

First Lecture, Heidelberg, January 21, 1909 1
"The Principle of Spiritual Economy in
Connection with Questions of Reincarnation: An
Aspect of the Spiritual Guidance of Mankind"

Second Lecture, Berlin, February 15, 1909 12
"Christianity in Human Evolution, Leading
Individualities and Avatar Beings"

Third Lecture, Munich, March 7, 1909 32
"More Intimate Aspects of Reincarnation"

Fourth and Fifth Lectures, Rome, March 29 and 31,
1909 56
"Results of Spiritual Scientific Investigations
of the Evolution of Humanity"

Sixth Lecture, Malsch, April 6, 1909 70
"On the Occasion of the Dedication of the
Francis of Assisi Branch"

Seventh Lecture, Cologne, April 10, 1909 89
"The Macrocosmic and Microcosmic Fire.
The Spiritualization of Breath and Blood"

Eighth Lecture, Cologne, April 11, 1909 101
"The Event of Golgotha. The Brotherhood of
the Holy Grail. The Spiritualized Fire"

Ninth Lecture, Kristiania (Oslo), May 16, 1909 117
  "Ancient Revelations and Learning: How to
  Ask Modern Questions"
Tenth Lecture, Berlin, May 25, 1909 123
  "The God of the Alpha and the God of the
  Omega"
Eleventh Lecture, Budapest, May 31, 1909 140
  "From Buddha to Christ"
Notes 157
Rudolf Steiner on the Transcriptions of Lectures 162

Introduction

1909 was the year when Rudolf Steiner published *Knowledge of the Higher World and Its Attainment* and completed *An Outline of Occult Science*, the sequel to his important book *Theosophy*, which had appeared in 1904. These three works, along with the earlier *Philosophy of Spiritual Activity* (1894), contain the nucleus of Steiner's anthroposophical thought.

The eleven lectures translated in this book were also given in 1909 and have been taken from the first half of a volume of lectures published in German under the title *Das Prinzip der spirituellen Ökonomie im Zusammenhang mit Wiederverkörperungsfragen. Ein Aspekt der geistigen Führung der Menschheit* (Rudolf Steiner Verlag: Dornach, Switzerland, 1979). The titles of this German volume and its component lectures are not by Rudolf Steiner but were assigned later on the basis of expressions used by him. Inasmuch as individual lectures in the German language have been published individually, their titles go back to the Complete Edition (CE) of Steiner's works begun by Marie Steiner. Steiner himself first spoke about the "principle of spiritual economy" in Berlin in 1908 when he was already working on his book *An Outline of Occult Science*.

The theme "spiritual economy" is directly related to Steiner's investigations about "the spiritual guidance of human beings and humanity" and later lectures dealing with karma. The eleven lectures translated in this book and the ten lectures translated and published under the title *Esoteric Rosicrucianism* (Anthroposophic Press: Spring Valley,

N.Y., 1978) occupy a special place in Rudolf Steiner's work because the aspect stressed in the two volumes is not presented in this fashion elsewhere in the Complete Edition. The Anthroposophical Society was founded as a separate organization in 1912, but Steiner did not actively guide it until 1923, two years before his death. At the time when the following lectures were given, Rudolf Steiner was still General Secretary of the German Section of the Theosophical Society and was using the terms "theosophy" and "theosophical," but always in the sense of the anthroposophical spiritual science presented by him from the beginning. He suggested later that these designations be replaced by "anthroposophy," "spiritual science," "anthroposophical," or "spiritual scientific."

As the excerpt from his autobiography printed at the end of this book indicates, Rudolf Steiner directed his lectures largely to individuals who were somewhat familiar with the rudiments of anthroposphical teachings and who joined him in the struggle and labor. Then, as he listened "to the pulsations in the soul-life of the members," the form of a lecture began to emerge. This process—admirable in itself—is problematic for the translator of Steiner's lectures because the style, syntax, and choice of words were intended to involve the souls of a listening, and not a reading, audience in a process of discovery.

Another problem facing the translator is the fact that most of the lectures collected were originally transcribed from Steiner's shorthand notes by different individuals and that the quality or completeness of these transcriptions differs considerably. Most can be considered nearly literal transcriptions of the spoken word, but in this book there seems to be gaps in the fourth, fifth, and ninth lectures. The reader should take into consideration that these three lectures were extracted from lecture cycles whose transcription was of insufficient quality to warrant their publication as a whole. The three seemingly incomplete lectures mentioned above were included in the present collection because they contain important details relevant to the subject matter and are not mentioned in other lectures. Finally, although the sixth lecture, given at the dedication ceremony of the Francis of Assisi Branch, seems repetitive and somewhat tedious, it too offers insights that add to the understanding of the theme.

Given these special circumstances I have tried to grasp the connotative quality of words, phrases, and sentences as Steiner used them in his probing, searching manner and render them in an English form that is simultaneously comprehensible and suggestive to a modern American speaker. Ultimately, however, such an attempt must not be considered more than an approximation of the author's original sense and a confirmation of Wilhelm von Humbolt's dictum that "all understanding is also a misunderstanding."

The translation of some words in this book may require an explanation. Throughout the eleven lectures I have endeavored to translate the German word *Mensch*, which has a masculine grammatical gender, not with "man" and in the plural with "men," but with "human being," choosing "human beings" when the repeated use of the reflexive pronouns "himself" and "herself" would seem awkward. I employed this practice in deference to modern female readers and because I wanted to dispel even the slightest hint of a mistaken notion arising from the use of "man" or "men" that human evolution and the reincarnation of the human soul applies primarily to males. One of the few exceptions to this practice is the rendering of *Geistesmensch* or *Geistmensch* as "spirit man," because "spirit human being" would sound awkward.

I capitalized Spiritual Science, an approximation of the German word *Geisteswissenschaft*, because I wanted to give the term greater prominence in a text that abounds with words related to spirit and because I consider it a proper noun that designates systematic anthroposophical thought and spiritual activity. At no place in the lectures does Rudolf Steiner use the word *Geisteswissenschaft* in its more widely known academic meaning of "humanities" or "liberal arts."

Furthermore, I rendered *Ätherleib* as "etheric body," rather than the "ether body" preferred by some translators because the word "ether" may conjure up distracting connotations in the minds of some and also because adjectival consistency of the term with the related concepts "physical" and "astral" (body) seemed to be desirable. On the other hand, I was reluctant to, but finally did, choose "ego" for German *Ich*, which in English can mean "I" or "self." Steiner once described the ego as "that which says 'I' to itself," but once, in the first lecture of the present book, he uses both *Ich* and "ego" to designate the same entity in different physical bodies. I felt that even though the current use of "ego" in psychology and popular speech can conjure up imprecise and misleading feelings, it is nevertheless a term to which many modern American readers ascribe a soul quality. Whenever Steiner uses the word *Ich*, which I have rendered in these lectures with "ego," it should be understood to mean the fourth body or principle with which the human being has been endowed—the other three being the physical, the etheric, and the astral bodies.

The few footnotes that were deemed necessary to provide some background information to the reader not familiar with certain historical personalities or contexts have been placed at the end of the book. Although I am sympathetic to the argument that the constant flipping of pages in search of a footnote can be distracting, I felt that the overriding concern should be that the reader gets a sense of the uninterrupted flow of thoughts with which Rudolf Steiner managed to involve his audience in the substance and dynamics of his presentations.

The lectures presented in this book touch on the very core of Rudolf Steiner's teachings and visions, according to which four basic facts govern human evolution from prehistoric times to the present. First, humanity has evolved as a result of the dialectics between forces and counterforces in the spiritual world. Second, earthly lives are repeated in a variety of spiritual ways, and valuable components are preserved for later use. Third, evolutionary forces have changed human consciousness, and new soul qualities are developed at certain intervals. Finally, the Mystery of Golgotha is the centerpiece of human evolution, but the influence of Christ-Impulse was manifest long before the birth of Jesus and can be observed in individualities such as Buddha, Zarathustra, and Moses.

Anthroposophy is not a religion—it goes beyond that—but its totality is subsumed under Rudolf Steiner's Christology. The reader will encounter recurring questions in these lectures—sometimes in a fresh combination, sometimes in a slightly different context, always thought provoking. For example, What is Spiritual Science and what can it do for us? What is human thought from a spiritual scientific point of view? How can it be that the Event at Golgotha is the centerpiece of all human evolution? Who was the Christ from an anthroposphical perspective, and how did the Christ-Impulse evolve? Why do the teachings of Zarathustra and Buddha constitute a transition in human consciousness and what, from an anthroposophical perspective, is the fundamental difference between the Buddhist and the Christian interpretation of life? How has the etheric body of Shem been preserved in all the Hebrew people? In what way does spiritual economy provide for certain etheric and astral bodies to remain active for the benefit of humanity, and what is the function of an avatar? Finally, why are we in the modern era, destined to undergo the complete unfolding of the ego?

It was Steiner's firm belief that his listeners or readers should never follow the teachings of anthroposophy blindly, but that they would have to struggle to find answers and new questions about the origin and the destiny of humanity. The seriousness of such a struggle gradually gives comfort to the human soul, and it is hoped that reading these lectures will have the same effect.

Peter Mollenhauer
Southern Methodist University

Lecture I

The Principle of Spiritual Economy in Connection with Questions of Reincarnation: An Aspect of the Spiritual Guidance of Mankind

Heidelberg, January 21, 1909

We shall discuss a few intimate questions of reincarnation that can be examined only in a circle of well prepared anthroposophists. By this we mean not only that they should be well prepared in theoretical knowledge but also that they have developed their sensitive faculty by working with others in a branch. For we all remember that our perceptions and sensibilities for truth have changed by virtue of this collaboration. What today we do not merely believe but perceive as truths that are *beyond* the realm of faith used to be incredible to us in earlier days and today still appears as fantastic nonsense or reverie to outsiders. Thus it is an indication of advancement if people have become accustomed to really living in these perceptions for only then can they begin to consider special questions. Much of what will be mentioned here seems to be remote, and yet even though we will first have to go back to far-distant periods of human evolution, all these things have an enlightening effect on our understanding of life and its phenomena. We must start by putting before our souls how the process of reincarnation takes place in general.

When human beings pass through the portal of death, they first have certain experiences. Their first experience is

1

the feeling that they are growing larger or that they are growing out of their skin. This has the effect of the human being attaining another perception of things than was the case earlier in physical life. Everything in the physical world has its definite place—either here or there—outside the observer, but that is not so in this new world. There, it is as if the human being were inside the objects, extended with or within them, whereas earlier he or she was only a separate object in its own place. The second experience after death consists of a human being's attaining a "memory tableau" of the life just completed, so that all events in it recur in comprehensive memory. This process lasts a definite amount of time. For reasons that cannot be stated here today, the duration of this memory is shorter or longer, depending on the individual. In general, the duration of this state can be determined from the length of time each human being was able to stay awake during the past life, continuously and without once succumbing to the forces of sleep. Supposing that the outer limit for a person's staying awake continuously had been forty-eight hours, then the memory tableau after death will also be forty-eight hours. And thus, this stage is like an overview of the past life.

Then the etheric body leaves the astral body, in which the ego is living. All three had been connected from the time they left the physical corpse, but now the etheric body separates itself from the other two and becomes an etheric corpse. However, today's human beings do not lose their etheric body completely but take an extract or excerpt along with them for all the times to follow. So in this sense the etheric corpse is cast off, but the fruit of the last life is carried along by the astral body and by the ego. If we want to be quite precise, we will have to say that something is taken along from the physical body as well: a kind of spiritual abstract of this body—the tincture medieval mystics spoke about. However, this abstract of the physical being is the

2

same in all lives; it merely represents the fact that the ego had been embodied. On the other hand, the essence of the etheric body is different in all lives, depending on what one has experienced in a life and on the degree of one's progress in it.

There follows the condition of what is called *kamaloca*, the time of weaning the soul from the effects of physical, sensuous existence, which lasts about a third of the time of a person's physical life. After the etheric body has been cast off, the astral body still contains all the passions, desires, and so on that it had at the end of life; they must be lost and purified, and that is *kamaloca*. Then the astral body is cast off and here, too, the fruit, the astral essence, is taken along; but the rest—the astral corpse—dissolves into the astral world. The human being now enters *devachan* where he or she prepares in the spiritual world for a new life in the future. Here human beings live with spiritual events and beings until they are again called into the physical world, be it because the karma of a person demands it or because an individual is needed on the physical earth.

This is a general description of the process. However, life in the spiritual realm progresses steadily in that the future joins itself to the past, and coming events are shaped with the help of past events. If one considers the details of this process, there is much among the wondrous things that become apparent, which is not contained in a simple presentation of the process of reincarnation. It is, after all, clear that great differences exist when one looks at the course of human development and that the extracts or abstracts of their bodies can have different values depending on the kinds of fruit they were able to extract from life. And when we remember that there are great leaders of humanity, initiates who lead other human beings into the spiritual worlds, then we have to ask ourselves this question: What causes the accomplishments of the initiates to be preserved for the future? External history is, of course, incapable of providing an answer to this question. What we have to do is scrutinize the reincarnation of the initiates and then apply the results of our investigation. We will begin with the oldest initiates.

Before humanity inhabited the continents as we know them today, the physiognomy of the earth was quite different. The area that is today covered by the Atlantic Ocean used to be the continent of Atlantis, which was destroyed by great catastrophes, as is reported by many peoples in their "saga of the great flood." The Atlanteans—and that is we ourselves—had their great leaders and initiates, and even in those days there existed places of instruction or schools where the initiates taught. The existence of these schools can be verified today by clairvoyant investigation. A good name for these schools where the leaders taught and lived is the word "oracle." the most important leader lived in one of the largest and most important oracles—the Sun Oracle. His main task consisted of revealing the secrets of the SUN —not the physical, external sun, but the real SUN. The latter consists of spiritual beings who make use of the physical sun much in the same way as human beings make use of the earth. To perceive and reveal the inner secrets of this Sun-existence was the task of the Great Sun Oracle. For it, sun light was not something physical, but rather every ray of sunshine represented the deed of the spiritual beings who reside on the sun. These great beings were exclusively on the sun during the time of ancient Atlantis. Later, when the great Being who was to be called the Christ united with the earth, this was no longer the case. Therefore, one can also call the Sun Oracle the Christ Oracle. The unification of the Christ-Being with the earth took place when the blood flowed from the wounds of Jesus Christ at Golgotha. That is when His essence united with the atmosphere of the earth, as can be perceived even today in clairvoyant retrospection. That is how the Christ-Being came down from the Sun to earth. When the light of spiritual illumination fell on Saul-Paul near Damascus, Paul beheld the Christ that was united with the earth and knew immediately that it was He who had shed His blood at Golgotha.

The sun oracle of ancient Atlantis had already prophesied the coming of Christ, of the Sun-God. To be sure, he was named the Christ only much later, but we can still say that the Sun Oracle is the Christ Oracle. These oracles had many successors in later periods, such as the Jupiter, Mars, Venus, Mercury, and Vulcan oracles, each with its great mysteries and teachings. Toward the end of the Atlantean era a group of advanced human beings was formed in the vicinity of what is today Ireland. The Great Leader chose a few from their midst who should carry on cultural life when the impending catastrophe would finally take place. However, enormous migrations had taken place a long time before to the continents of Europe, Asia, and Africa, which were beginning to rise out of the sea. Many successors of the old oracles came into being on these continents, but not without gradually losing the significance of the old oracles. The Great Leader, however, chose the best people in order to lead them into a special land. They were plain and simple people who were different from most other Atlanteans in that they had almost completely lost their clairvoyance. You will remember that the majority of the Atlanteans were clairvoyant. When they fell asleep at night, they did not lose consciousness, but rather the sense world disappeared and there arose in its place the spiritual world in which they were the companions of divine-spiritual beings. The advanced people in Atlantis had begun to develop their intellect, yet they were simple people who possessed inner warmth and were deeply devoted to their leader. He took this select group East to the center of Asia, where he founded the center of the post-Atlantean culture. After the group had arrived in central Asia, it was

5

kept in isolation from the human beings who were unsuited to the task. The descendants of this group were educated with special care, and only they developed the qualities necessary to make them great teachers. All this happened in a mysterious way. It was the task of the Manu, the Great Leader, to make the necessary preparations for preserving for the new race everything that was good in the Atlantean culture and thus to lay the foundation for the progression of a new culture. The sages living in the smaller oracles were unable to devote themselves to this task because only the Manu had preserved from the great initiates of the oracles that which we call the etheric body. As we have seen, this etheric body normally dissolves as the second corpse, but in certain cases it was preserved. The greatest of these sages in the oracles had worked so much into their etheric bodies that the latter had become too valuable simply to be dissipated into the general etheric world. Therefore, the seven best etheric bodies belonging to the seven greatest initiates were preserved until the Manu had developed the seven most outstanding people from his group in such a way that they were suited to absorb the preserved etheric bodies. Only the etheric body of the Great Initiate of the Christ Oracle was, in a certain sense, treated differently from the others. And so the seven sages, or Rishis, who had received the seven etheric bodies of the greatest initiates, went to India, where they became the founders and great teachers of Indian culture.

This very ancient, holy culture of the pre-Vedic era originated from the seven Rishis who bore the preserved etheric bodies of the initiates of the various oracles, such as Venus, Jupiter, Mars, and so on. In a way, a copy of those initiates, a repetition of their capabilities, came to be at work in these Rishis, even though they were plain and simple people when seen from the outside. Their significance was not evident from their external appearance, nor was their intellect

6

commensurate with the loftiness of their prophecies. Possessing their own astral bodies and egos but being endowed with the etheric bodies of those great sages, these Rishis were not scholars and did not rank so highly in terms of their power of judgment as did many of their contemporaries, or even as many people in our times. But in inspired ages they were, in a way, seized upon by these oracle beings whose etheric bodies became active in them. In that sense they were only instruments through whom that ancient wisdom was proclaimed—those Vedas that are far too difficult, if not incomprehensible, for human beings in our age. And this is how the old wisdom of the ancient oracles was revealed, with the exception of the Sun, or Christ, Oracle which could not be completely revealed in such a way. Only a faint reflection of the Sun-wisdom could be transmitted because it was so lofty that even the Holy Rishis could not grasp it.

We can see here that reincarnation does not always proceed as smoothly and in such general ways as is often supposed. Rather, if an etheric body is especially valuable, it is —to express it metaphorically—preserved like a mold that can be imprinted on human beings of later ages. Such an occurrence is not all that rare, and many a plain person can have an extremely valuable etheric body that is preserved for later use. Not all etheric bodies dissolve after death, but some of those that are especially useful are transferred to other human beings. But the "I" of the individual receiving the etheric or astral body is not at all identical with the ego of the donor. Disregarding this fact can easily lead to great misconceptions on the part of someone who investigates a human being's past with faulty clairvoyant methods. It is for this reason that the occult theories about the earlier lives of human beings are often completely wrong, just as it would be wrong to say that the seven Rishis had the same egos as the initiates whose etheric bodies they had received.

Only when we know such things can we gain clarity

about much that is important in human evolution, such as the preservation of human achievements for nature's economy. It is through the transmission of these seven etheric bodies that the highest values of the Atlantean culture were saved and preserved for posterity.

Let us discuss another example, which could not be mentioned earlier, and look at the ancient Persian time, the period of Zarathustra's culture.[1] We consider it an important period because it was the first post-Atlantean time in which greater emphasis was placed on the conquest of the physical world. During the Indian epoch, the longing for the spiritual realm dominated the thinking of human beings. Most of them considered the spiritual world as being real and felt like strangers in the physical realm, which to them was transitory, illusory, *maya*.[2] This consciousness changed in the prehistoric Persian culture through the teachings of Zarathustra, that is to say the teachings of the original and first Zarathustra, because there were many Zarathustras after him. His task as a leader was to draw the attention of human beings to the physical plane, to make inventions, manufacture instruments and tools, and thus to conquer the physical world. This was necessary because human beings had to become acquainted with the physical world as something that was important to them. However, the tempter within a human being tells him or her that the physical is the only reality and that there exists nothing beyond the earthly realm. This belief, Zarathustra teaches, is false because behind the physical there is the spiritual world, just as the physical sun is for us the external sign of the great Sun-Being, of the Spiritual-Divine, of the Great Aura, of Ahura Mazdao, of Ormuzd. These names designate a Being that is now physically invisible and lives far away from the earth on the sun. But, as goes Zarathustra's teaching, some day this Being will reveal Itself; later It will make Its appearance on earth, just as It is now present on the sun.

Zarathustra initiated his most intimate students into

these mysteries, but the most profound teachings he imparted to two of them. The first one was primarily instructed in everything that concerns human judgment, such as natural science, astronomy and astrology, agriculture, and other disciplines. All this knowledge was transmitted to this one disciple by a secret process of communication between the two. This prepared the disciple in such a way that in the following reincarnation he was able to carry the astral body of his teacher; and he was reincarnated as Hermes,[3] the great teacher and sage of the Egyptian Mysteries. Born with Zarathustra's astral body, Hermes became the bearer of the great wisdom.

The second intimate disciple was instructed in the subject matters that express themselves especially in the etheric body and are deeper in substance. This disciple received in the following incarnation the etheric body of Zarathustra. The stories about this in religious documents are comprehensible only through these explanations. At his reincarnation, the student had to be animated in a very special way, that is the etheric body had to be strong before the astral body could be awakened. That could be achieved through the circumstances surrounding the birth of this reincarnated disciple, who was none other than Moses. The fact that he was placed into a box made of bulrushes that was allowed to float on the water and so on had the purpose of awakening completely the etheric body of the child. That enabled Moses to survey in his memory times long past, to pictorially record the genesis of the earth, and to read in the Akasha Chronicle.[4] And, thus, one sees that these things are at work behind the scenes, as it were, and that through this process everything valuable is preserved and re-utilized.

There are other examples from later times, for example Nicholas of Cusa (Cusanus),[5] a curious personality of the fifteenth century. Here we can see the interesting case of how the research of this man, as it were, laid the groundwork for the entire body of the teaching of Copernicus,[6] who lived in the sixteenth century. To be sure, this body of teaching is not yet quite as ripe in Cusa's books as in those written by Copernicus, but they contain all the essential ideas, a fact that confounds most traditional scholars. The fact is that the astral body of Cusa was transferred to Copernicus even though the ego of the latter was different from that of Cusa. This is how Copernicus received the foundation and all the preparations for his own doctrine.

Similar cases occur often. What is especially valuable is always preserved; nothing vanishes. But this fact also enhances the possibility of error in any attempt to establish correspondences, especially when people attempt to investigate the earlier lives of a human being with the help of a medium in séance. The transfer of an etheric or astral body to a human being in more modern times usually happens now in such a way that an astral body is transferred to a member of the same language group, whereas an etheric body can be transferred to a member of another language group.

When a pioneering personality dies, his or her etheric body is always preserved, and occult schools have always known the artifical methods by which this was accomplished. Considering now another characteristic case, we can say that it was important for certain purposes in the more modern age that the etheric body of Galileo[7] should be preserved. He was the great reformer of mechanical physics whose accomplishments were so tremendous that one can say many of the purely practical accomplishments of the modern age would not have come about without his discoveries, for all technical progress rests on Galileo's science. The tunnels of St. Gotthart or Simplon have become possible only because Leibniz,[8] Newton,[9] and Galileo developed the sciences of integral and differential calculus, mechanics, and so on. With regard to Galileo, it would have been a waste in nature's economy had his etheric body, the carrier of his memory and talent, been lost. And that is why his etheric body was transferred to another human being: Michail Lomonosov,[10] who came from a poor Russian village and was later to become the founder of Russian grammar and classical literature. Lomonosov, however, is not the reincarnated Galileo, as might be supposed as a result of superficial investigation.

And thus we see that there are many such cases and that the process of reincarnation is not so simple as most people of our time think. If, therefore, people investigate earlier incarnations with the help of occult methods, they have to exercise much greater caution. In many instances, it is nothing but childishness if people state or imagine they are the reincarnated such and such, perhaps Nero, Napoleon, Beethoven, or Goethe. Such silly things must, of course, be rejected. But the matter becomes more dangerous when advanced occultists make mistakes in this regard and imagine that they are the reincarnation of this or that man, when in fact they carry only his etheric body. Not only is this an error that is regrettable in itself, but the human being coming to these conclusions would live under the influence of this mistaken idea, and that would have nearly catastrophic consequences. The result of such an illusion would be that the whole development of the soul proceeds in the wrong direction.

We have seen not only that the egos are capable of reincarnation, but that the lower members of the human constitution in a certain sense undergo a similar process. The result of this is that the whole configuration of the process of reincarnation is much more complicated than is usually supposed. And thus we see that the ego of Zarathustra was reincarnated as Zarathas—Nazarathos, who in turn became the teacher of Pythagoras.[11] On the other hand, Zarathustra's astral body reappeared in Hermes and his etheric body in Moses. Therefore, nothing is lost in the world; everything is preserved and transmitted to posterity, provided it is valuable enough.

Lecture II

Christianity in Human Evolution: Leading
Individualities and Avatar Beings

Berlin, February 25, 1909

You will have been able to see from the one lecture given
here on the more complicated question of reincarnation that
the spiritual scientific view of the world continues its progression. Hence, what in the beginning could be presented
as elementary truths is undergoing a metamorphosis, so that
gradually we rise to ever higher truths. It is therefore correct
to present general cosmic truths in their initial stage in as
simple and elementary a form as possible. Thereafter, however, it is also necessary to advance slowly from the simple
ABC's to the higher truths, because you will agree that
through these higher truths we gradually attain what Spiritual Science intends to give us: the opportunity to understand and penetrate the very world that surrounds us in the
sentient—the physical—sphere. Now it is true that we have
a long way to go in our ascent before we shall be able to
somehow draw the connecting links in the spiritual lines
and forces that exist behind the world of the senses. But you
will agree that this or that phenomenon in our existence has
become clearer and easier to explain just by what we have
been discussing in the last few lectures. So today we want to
advance a little in this specific area and again take as our
subject matter the more complicated questions of reincarnation—of reembodiment.

Above all, we want to see clearly that there are differences among the beings who occupy leading positions in the human evolution of the earth. We have to distinguish such leading individualities in the course of human evolution who, as it were, developed from the beginning with humanity on this earth as it exists, but with the important distinction that they progressed more rapidly. We might put it this way: If we go back in time to the most ancient Lemurian Age, we find the most varied stages of development among the human beings then incarnated. All the souls incarnated at that time have been repeatedly reincarnated—reembodied—during the successive Atlantean and post-Atlantean periods. The speed with which these souls developed varied. Some souls are alive that developed relatively slowly as they went through various incarnations; they still have long distances to traverse in the future. But then there are also those souls who have developed rapidly and who, one might say, have utilized their incarnations in a more productive way. They are now on a high plane of soul-spiritual development, one that will be reached by normal human beings only in the far-distant future. But as we dwell on this sphere of soul life, we can nevertheless say this: No matter how advanced these individual souls may be, however far they may tower above normal human beings, yet within our earthly evolution they have made a journey similar to the rest of humanity, except that they have advanced more rapidly.

In addition to these leading individualities, who in this sense are like other human beings but stand on a higher plane, there are also other individualities—other beings—who have not gone through various incarnations as have the other human beings in the course of human evolution. We can visualize what lies at the bottom of this when we tell ourselves the following: There have been beings in the time of the Lemurian evolution under consideration—beings who no longer needed to descend into physical embodiment as the other human beings just described. They were beings capable of accomplishing their development in higher, more spiritual realms who did not need to descend into corporeal bodies for their further progress. However, in order to intervene in the course of human evolution, such beings can nevertheless descend vicariously into corporeal bodies such as our own. Thus it can happen that such a being appears; if we test it clairvoyantly in regard to the soul, we cannot say, as we can of other human beings, that we trace it back in time and discover it in a previously fleshly incarnation, then trace it farther back and find it again in another incarnation, and so on. Instead, we will have to admit that in tracing the soul of such a being back through the course of time, we may not arrive at an earlier fleshly incarnation of such a being at all. However, if we do, it is only because the being is able to descend repeatedly in certain intervals in order to incarnate vicariously in a human body.

Such a spiritual being who descends in this way into a human body in order to intervene in evolution as a human being is called an "avatar" in the East; such a being gains nothing from this embodiment for himself and experiences nothing that is of significance for the world. This, then, is the distinction between a leading being that has emanated from human evolution and beings whom we call avatars. The latter reap no benefit for themselves from their physical embodiments, or even from one embodiment to which they subject themselves; they enter a physical body for the blessing and progress of all human beings. To repeat—an avatar being can enter a human body just once or several times in succession; but when it does, it is then something different from any other human individuality.

The greatest avatar being who has lived on earth, as you can gather from the spirit of our lectures here, is the Christ —the Being whom we designated as the Christ, and who took possession of the body of Jesus of Nazareth when he

14

was thirty years of age. This Being, who did not come into contact with our earth until the beginning of our era, was incarnated for three years in a body of flesh and has since that time been in contact with the astral, i.e., the spiritual, sphere of our supersensible world; this Being has a unique significance as an avatar being. Although other, lower avatar beings can reincarnate several times, it would be in vain for us to seek the Christ-Being in an earlier human embodiment on earth. The difference between the Christ and the lower avatars does not lie in the fact that the latter incarnate repeatedly, but that they derive no benefits for themselves from their earthly embodiments. Human beings give the world nothing; they only take from it. By contrast, these beings only give; they take nothing from the earth. To gain a perfect understanding of this idea, you have to distinguish between such a lofty avatar being as the Christ and lower avatar beings. Such avatar beings can have the most varied missions on earth; and in discussing one of those missions, we want to avoid speculative language and take a concrete case as an illustration for such a mission.

You all know from the ancient Hebrew story of Noah that a large part of post-Atlantean, post-Noah humanity traces its ancestry back to the three sons of Noah—Shem, Ham, and Japhet. It is not our purpose today to elucidate what Noah and these three tribal ancestors represent in other respects. We simply want to elucidate here that Hebrew literature, speaking of Shem as one of Noah's sons, traces the whole tribe of the Semites back to him as its ancestor. A genuinely occult perception of such a matter, of such a story, is always grounded in deeper truths. Those who are able to conduct occult research into such things know the following about Shem, the ancestor of the Semites.

When such a personality is destined to become the forefather of an entire tribe, care must be taken from his birth—and even earlier—to insure that he can become such a fore-

15

bear. Now, what preparations were necessary to ensure that an individuality such as Shem could indeed become the forefather of a whole people or tribal community? In the case of Shem it was done by giving him a quite specially prepared etheric body. We know that when human beings are born into this world, they structure around their individuality an etheric or life body, along with the other members of their being. A special etheric being must somehow be prepared for the ancestor of a tribe because it has to be, as it were, the prototype of an etheric body for all the descendants in succeeding generations. And so it happens that we have in such a tribal individuality a typical etheric body, a prototype as it were. Because of blood relationship in successive generations, the etheric bodies of all descendants of the tribe are in a certain sense copies of the ancestor's etheric body. Thus, every Semitic person's etheric body had something like a copy of Shem's etheric body woven into it. Now, by what means is such a condition brought about in the course of human evolution?

Let us look at Shem more carefully. We find that his etheric body received its archetypal form because an avatar had woven himself into it. It was not such a high avatar that we can compare him with other avatar beings, but still a lofty avatar descended into his etheric body. This avatar individuality was not connected with Shem's astral body nor with his ego, however, but was woven into his etheric body alone. From this example we can study what it means when an avatar being partakes in the constitution and composition of a human being. What does it mean, then, when a human being who, like Shem, has the mission to be the ancestor of a whole people should in a way have the essence of an avatar woven into his body? It means that every time the essence of an avatar is woven into the soul of a fleshly being, any one member—or even several members—of the supersensible

16

constitution of this human being are capable of being multiplied and split into many parts.

The fact that an avatar being was interwoven with Shem's etheric body made it possible for countless copies of the original to come into being and to be woven into all the human beings who became the descendants of this ancestor in subsequent generations. Thus, the descent of an avatar being is, among other things, significant in that it contributes to the multiplication of one or several members of the being who is animated by the avatar. As you can see from this, an especially precious etheric body was present in Shem, an archetypal etheric body, prepared by an exalted avatar and then woven into Shem so that it could descend in many copies to all those who were destined for consanguinity with him.

As we have already said in a previous lecture, a spiritual economy exists by virtue of the fact that something of special value is preserved and carried over into the future. We have heard not only that the ego reincarnates but also that the astral body and the etheric body are capable of doing the same. Aside from the fact that countless copies of Shem's etheric body came into being, his own etheric body was also preserved in the spiritual world because it could later be useful in the mission of the Hebrew people. Remember that all the peculiarities of the Hebrews had originally come to expression in this etheric body, and if at any time something of special importance was to happen to them—if one of them should be assigned a special task or mission, then this could be best accomplished by an individual who bore the etheric body of the ancestor within himself. As a matter of fact, an individual bearing the etheric body of Shem later played an important part in the history of the Hebrew people. We have here indeed one of those wonderous complications in the evolution of humankind that can explain so much to us. We are dealing here with an exalted individuality who, as it were, was compelled to condescend in order to be able to speak to the Hebrews in a comprehensible manner and to give them the strength necessary for a special mission. By analogy, if an intellectually advanced individual had to speak to a primitive tribe, he would have to learn its language, but this does not mean that the language in question would elevate him personally; all the individual would have to do is to take the trouble of acquainting himself with the language. In this same way, an exalted individuality had to make a strong personal effort to become one with Shem's etheric body to be able to give a definite impulse to the ancient Hebrew people. This personality was the very Melchizedek[12] you find in Biblical history. In a way, he wore Shem's etheric body so that later he could give Abraham the impulse that you find so beautifully in the Bible. What was contained in the individuality of Shem was multiplied because an avatar being was incarnated in it, and all this became interwoven with all the other etheric bodies of the Hebrews. In addition, Shem's own etheric body was preserved in the spiritual world so that it could be borne at a later time by Melchizedek, who was to give the Hebrews an important impulse through Abraham.

This is how finely interwoven the facts behind the physical world are, facts that are needed to elucidate to us what happens in the physical world. Only by being able to point to such facts of a spiritual nature that are behind the facts of the physical world do we learn to interpret history. History can never become comprehensible through considering physical facts alone.

Now, if the descent of an avatar being affects the soul-spiritual components of the human being in that he or she becomes the bearer of the avatar's soul, and if this results in multiplication and transmission of the archetypal copy onto others, then this phenomenon becomes especially significant with the appearance of Christ on earth. Because the avatar essence of Christ lived in the body of Jesus of Nazareth, it became possible not only that the etheric body but also that the astral body and even that the ego were multiplied innumerable times; by ego, I mean the "I" as an impulse that was kindled in the astral body of Jesus of Nazareth when Christ entered his threefold sheath. However, foremost in our consideration is here the fact that the etheric and astral bodies could be multiplied because of the presence of the avatar being.

Now, one of the most significant turning points in human history was the appearance of the Christ principle in earthly evolution. What I have told you about Shem is actually typical and characteristic of pre-Christian times. When an etheric or an astral body is multiplied in this way, the copies of the original are usually transmitted to those people who are related by blood to the ancestor who had the prototype. Hence, the copies of Shem's etheric body were transmitted to the members of the Hebrew tribe, but when the Christ Avatar Being appeared, all this was changed. The etheric and astral bodies of Jesus of Nazareth were multiplied and the copies preserved until they could be used in the course of human evolution. However, they were not bound up with this or that nationality or tribe. But when in the course of time a human being appeared who, irrespective of nationality, was mature and suitable enough to have his own etheric or astral body interwoven with a copy of the etheric or astral body of Jesus of Nazareth, then those bodies could be woven into that particular person's being. Thus we see how it became possible in the course of time for all kinds of people to have copies of the astral or etheric body of Jesus of Nazareth woven into their souls.

The intimate history of Christian development is connected with this fact. What is normally described as the history of Christian development is a sum of entirely external

19

occurrences. It is for this reason that far too little attention is given to what is most important—the distinction of actual periods in Christian development. Anyone who can look more deeply into the developmental progress of Christianity will easily perceive that the manner in which Christianity was disseminated was different in the first few centuries from that of later centuries in the Christian era. In the first few Christian centuries the dissemination of Christianity was, in a way, bound up with everything that could be gained from the physical plane. We need only look at the early teachers of Christianity to see how they emphasized physical memories, physical connections, and everything that had remained in a physical state. Just consider how Irenaeus,[13] a man who contributed so much in the first century to the dissemination of Christian doctrine in various countries, stressed that memories should extend back to those who had listened to the disciples of the Apostles. It was important to prove through such physical recollections that Christ Himself had actually taught in Palestine. It was specially emphasized, for example, that Papias[14] himself had sat at the feet of the Apostles' disciples. Even the places were shown and described where such personalities had sat—people who could still be cited as eyewitnesses to the fact that Christ had lived in Palestine. The physical progress in memory was what was especially emphasized in the first few centuries of Christianity.

How much stress remained on everything that was physical can be seen from the words of the old St. Augustine[15] living at the end of this era, who said: "Why do I believe in the truths of Christianity? Because the authority of the Catholic Church compels me to do so." To him, the physical authority's telling him that something exists in the physical world was the important and essential thing. The determining factor for him was that a corporate body had preserved itself within which one personality is linked back to another until one arrives at one who, like Peter, was a companion of

Christ. Hence, we can see that in the dissemination of Christianity during the early centuries, it was the documents and the impressions of the physical plane to which the greatest importance was given.

All that changes after the time of St. Augustine and into the tenth, eleventh, and twelfth centuries. It was then no longer possible to appeal to living memories or to consult the documents of the physical plane because they were too far removed from the present. Something entirely different was present in the whole mood and the disposition of the human beings, especially the Europeans, who were then embracing Christianity. It was the feeling, the direct knowledge, of the existence of Christ, of His death on the cross, and of His continuing life. From the fourth and fifth up to the tenth and twelfth centuries, a large number of people would have considered it foolish to be told that they could doubt the events in Palestine because they knew better. People like these were especially common in European countries, and they had always been able to experience inwardly in miniature a kind of Pauline revelation, that is the experience through which Saul became Paul on the road to Damascus.

What made it possible for a number of people in those centuries to be able to receive revelations about the events in Palestine that were in a sense clairvoyant? It was possible because the multiplied copies of the etheric body of Jesus of Nazareth had been preserved and were in these centuries woven into the etheric bodies of a large number of people who wore these multiplied copies as one would wear a garment. Their etheric body did not consist entirely of the copy of Jesus' etheric body, but it had had woven into it a copy of the original. There were indeed human beings in those centuries who were able to have such an etheric body and who could thereby have an immediate knowledge of Jesus of Nazareth and the Christ.

All this, however, had the effect that the Christ image

21

was no longer associated with the externally historical and physical transmission of the story. The highest degree of such disassociation is evident in that wonderful literary work of the ninth century, the *Heliand*.[16] This poem was written down by a seemingly simple Saxon in the time of Louis the Pious, who reigned from 814-840. The Saxon's astral body and ego could not match what was in his etheric body because the latter had had woven into it a copy of the etheric body of Jesus of Nazareth. This simple Saxon priest, the author of the poem, was certain from immediate clairvoyant vision that the Christ existed on the astral plane and that He was the same Christ who had been crucified at Golgotha! And because this was a direct certainty for him, he no longer needed to resort to historical documents or to physical mediation in order to know that the Christ does exist. Therefore, he describes the Christ detached from the whole Palestinian setting and from the peculiarities of the Jewish character. This poet, then, depicts the Christ as if He were something like a leader of a Central European or Germanic tribe, and he describes those who surround Him as His followers—the Apostles—as if they were vassals of a Germanic prince. The entire external scenery has been changed, but the structure of the events and the essential and eternal aspects of the Christ figure remain the same. This poet did not have to hold rigidly to historical events when he was speaking of the Christ because he had a direct knowledge of Him that was built upon a foundation as important as a copy of the etheric body of Jesus of Nazareth. What he had acquired as immediate knowledge, he draped with a different external setting. Even as we have been able to describe this writer of the *Heliand* poem as one of the peculiar personalities who had a copy of the etheric body of Jesus of Nazareth woven into his own etheric body, we can find other personalities in this period who also carried a copy within themselves. We see, therefore, that the most important things take place behind the physical occurrences and that these things can explain history to us in an intimate way.

If we continue to trace Christian development, we come to the period from about the eleventh or twelfth up to the fifteenth century, and it is here that we discover an entirely different mystery that now carried evolution forward. If you remember, first it was the memory of what had taken place on the physical plane, followed by the etheric element being woven into the etheric bodies of the pillars of Christianity in Central Europe. But later, from the twelfth to the fifteenth century, it was numerous copies of the astral body of Jesus of Nazareth that became interwoven with the astral bodies of the most important pillars of Christianity. In those days the human beings had egos capable of forming extremely false ideas about all sorts of things, yet in their astral bodies a direct force of strength, of devotion, and of the immediate certainty of holy truths was alive. Such people possessed deep fervor, an absolutely direct conviction, and also in some circumstances the ability to prove this conviction. What sometimes must strike us as being so strange especially in these personalities is that their ego development was not at all equal to that of their astral bodies because the latter had copies of the astral body of Jesus Christ woven into them. Their ego behavior often seemed grotesque, but the world of their sentiments, feelings, and fervor was magnificent and exalted.

Francis of Assisi,[17] for example, was such a personality. We study his life and cannot, as modern people, understand what his conscious ego was; yet we cannot help having the most profound reverence for the richness and range of his feelings and for all that he did. This is no longer a problem once we adopt the perspective mentioned above. He was one of those who had a copy of the astral body of Jesus of Nazareth woven into their own astral bodies, and this en-

23

abled him to accomplish what he did. Many of his followers in the Order of the Franciscans, with its servants and minorites, had such copies interwoven with their astral bodies in a similar fashion.

All the strange and otherwise mysterious phenomena of that time will become lucid and clear to you as soon as you set this mediation in world evolution between that time and previous times properly before the eye of your soul. The important distinction that must be made for these people of the Middle Ages is whether what was woven into their souls from the astral body of Jesus of Nazareth contained more of what we call the sentient soul, more of the intellectual soul, or more of the consciousness soul. This distinction is important because, as you know, the astral body must be envisioned as containing, in a certain sense, all of these three components, as well as the ego, which it encompasses. What was woven into Francis of Assisi was, as it were, the sentient soul of Jesus of Nazareth, and the same is true in the case of that remarkable personality Elisabeth of Thüringen, who was born in 1207.[18] Knowing this secret of her life will enable you to follow the course of her life with your whole soul. She, too, was a personality who had a copy of the astral body of Jesus of Nazareth woven into her sentient soul. The riddle of the human being is solved for us by means of just such knowledge.

If you know that during this time the most diverse personalities had sentient soul, intellectual soul, or consciousness soul woven into them as copies of the astral body of Jesus of Nazareth, you will above all comprehend that little understood and much maligned science that has become known as scholasticism.[19] What tasks did the scholastics set for themselves? They set out to find, on the basis of judgment and intellect, verifications and proof of those phenomena for which historical links and physical mediation did not exist and which could no longer be known with the direct clairvoyant certainty possible in previous centuries through the interwoven etheric body of Jesus of Nazareth. These people set themselves the task by saying: Tradition has communicated to us that the Being known as Jesus Christ has appeared in history and that, in addition, other spiritual beings of whom religious documents bear witness have intervened in human religion. Then, from the intellectual soul, that is from the intellectual element of the copy of Jesus Christ's astral body, they set themselves the task of proving with subtle and clearly developed concepts all that their literature contained as mystery truths. Thus arose the strange science that attempted what was probably the most penetrating intellectual venture ever undertaken in the history of human thought. One may think of the content of scholasticism as one wishes, but for several centuries this school of thought developed the capacity of human reflection and thus put its imprint on the culture of the time. Scholasticism accomplished this by an extremely subtle discernment between and outlining of various concepts. As a result, between the thirteenth and fifteenth centuries the school implanted into humanity the capacity to think with acute and penetrating logic.

The special conviction that Christ can be found in the human ego arose among those who were imbued more strongly with the copy of the consciousness soul of Jesus of Nazareth, because the ego functions in the consciousness soul. Because these individuals had within them the element of consciousness soul from the astral body of Jesus of Nazareth, the inner Christ rose resplendent within their souls, and through this astral body they came to know that the Christ within them was the Christ Himself. These were the individuals whom you know as Meister Eckhart,[20] Johannes Tauler,[21] and all other pillars of medieval mysticism.

Here you see how the most diverse manifestations of the astral body, multiplied by the fact that the exalted Avatar

Being of the Christ had entered the body of Jesus of Nazareth, continued to work in the following age and brought about the real development of Christianity. This is an important transition in other respects as well. We have seen how humanity in the course of its evolution was otherwise dependent upon having incorporated within it these copies of the Jesus of Nazareth Being. In the early centuries people had existed who depended entirely on the physical plane; then in the following centuries there were human beings who were susceptible to having the etheric body of Jesus of Nazareth woven into their own etheric bodies. Later, human beings, one might say, became more oriented toward the astral body, and that is how the copy of the astral body of Jesus of Nazareth could now be incorporated into them. The astral body is the bearer of judgment, and it was the human capacity to judge that was awakened between the twelfth and the fourteenth centuries.

This awakening of the astral body can also be observed in another phenomenon. Before the twelfth century, the depths of mystery contained in the Holy Communion were especially well understood. It was not widely discussed, but rather was accepted in a manner that enabled a human being to feel everything that was contained in the words, "This is My body and this is My blood." Christ meant with these words that He would be united with the earth and become its planetary spirit. And because flour is the most precious thing on earth, bread became for human beings the body of Christ, and the sap flowing through plants and vines became to them something of His blood. Through this knowledge, the value of the Lord's Supper was not diminished but was, on the contrary, enhanced. People in the early centuries felt something of these infinite depths, and they continued to do so up to the time when the power of judgment was awakened in the astral body. It was only then that disputes began about the meaning of the Lord's Supper. Just think about the discussions about the meaning of the Lord's Supper among the Hussites, Lutherans, and the dissenting Zwinglians and Calvinists.[22] They would not have been possible in earlier times when people still had an immediate, direct knowledge of the Lord's Supper!

Here we see verified a great historical law that should be of special significance to the spiritual scientist: As long as people knew what the Lord's Supper was, they did not discuss it. They began to discuss it only after they had lost direct knowledge of it. Let us consider the fact that people discuss a particular matter as an indication that they do not really know it. Where knowledge exists, knowledge is narrated, and there is no particular desire for discussion. Where people feel like discussing something, they have, as a rule, no knowledge of the truth. Discussion begins only when there is a lack of knowledge, and it is always and everywhere the sign of decline regarding the seriousness of a subject matter when discussions about it are to be heard. Discussions portend the decline of a particular trend. It is very important that time and again in Spiritual Science we learn to understand that the wish to discuss something should actually be construed as a sign of ignorance. On the other hand, we should cultivate the opposite of discussion, and that is the will to learn and the will to gradually comprehend what is in question.

Here we see an important historical fact verified by the development of Christianity itself. But we can also learn something else when we see how, in the centuries of Christianity characterized above, the power of judgment, this keen intellectual wisdom, is further developed. Indeed, when we focus our attention on realities and not on dogmas, we can learn how much Christianity has accomplished since its inception. Take scholasticism. What has become of it when we look not at its content, but perceive it as a means of cultivating and disciplining our mental faculties? Do you want to know? Scholasticism has become modern natural science! The latter is inconceivable without the reality of medieval Christian science. It is not only that Copernicus was a canon and Giordano Bruno[23] a Dominican, but that all thought forms with which natural objects have been tackled since the fifteenth and sixteenth centuries are nothing but what was developed and nurtured by the Christian science of the Middle Ages from the eleventh through the sixteenth centuries. There are people today who look up passages in scholastic books, compare them with recent findings of natural history, and then say Haeckel and others aver something entirely different. Such people do not live in reality but in the world of abstractions! Realities are what matters! The work of Haeckel, Darwin, DuBois-Reymond, Huxley,[24] and others would all have been impossible had the Christian science of the Middle Ages not preceded them. These modern scientists owe their mode of thought to the Christian science of the Middle Ages. That is the reality, and it is from that science that humanity has learned to think in the true sense of the word.

But there is more. Read David Friedrich Strauss[25] and try to observe his mode of thinking. Try to realize what his chain of reasoning is: how he wants to present the entire life of Jesus of Nazareth as a myth. Do you know where the keenness of his thinking comes from? He gets it from the Christian science of the Middle Ages. Everything used today to combat Christianity so radically has been taken over from the Christian world of learning in the Middle Ages. Actually, today there cannot be an opponent of Christianity of whom it could not easily be shown that he would be unable to think as he does had he not learned his thought forms from the Christian science of the Middle Ages. If one considered that fact, one would indeed look at world history as it really is.

What, then, has happened since the sixteenth century?

Since that time the human ego has increasingly come into prominence and with it human egotism, and with egotism, materialism. Everything that the ego had absorbed and acquired was gradually unlearned and forgotten. Human beings now were compelled to limit themselves to what the ego could observe and to what the physical sensory system was able to give to the ordinary intelligence. That is all the ego could take into its inner sanctuary. Culture since the sixteenth century has become the culture of egotism.

What must now enter into the ego? Christian evolution has passed through a development in the physical, etheric, and astral bodies and has made its way as far as the ego. Now it must take into this ego the mysteries and secrets of Christianity itself. Following a time when the ego learned to think through Christianity and then apply the thoughts to the external world, it must now become possible for the ego to become a Christ-receptive organ. This ego must now rediscover the wisdom which is the primordial wisdom of the Great Avatar, of Christ Himself. And how is this to be done? It must be done through a more profound understanding of Christianity through Spiritual Science. Having been carefully prepared through the three stages of physical, etheric, and astral development, the inner organ would now have to open itself to its human host so that he or she could henceforth look into the spiritual environment with the eye that the Christ can open for us.

Christ descended to earth as the greatest avatar being. Let us view this in the right perspective and try to look at the world as we would be able to do after we have received the Christ into ourselves. Then we would find the whole process of our world evolution illuminated and pervaded by the Christ Being. That is to say, we would describe how the physical body of human beings originated on Old Saturn,[26] how the etheric body made its appearance on Old Sun, the astral body on Old Moon, and the ego on the Earth. Finally, we would find how everything tends toward the goal of becoming ever more independent and individual in order to incorporate into the evolution of the earth the very wisdom that passes from the Sun to the earth. In a way, Christ and Christianity must become the perspective center of a cosmic view for the liberated ego.

So you see how Christianity has gradually prepared itself for what it is to become. In the early centuries the Christian received Christianity with his physical ability to cognize truth, later with his etheric capacity, and throughout the Middle Ages with his astral capacity to cognize truth. Then Christianity in its true form was repressed for a while until the ego had been trained by the three bodies in the course of Christian evolution. But after this ego had learned how to think and direct its vision to the objective world, it is now mature enough to perceive in all phenomena of the objective world the spiritual facts that are so intimately linked with the Central Being, the Christ. Thus, the ego is now capable of beholding the Christ everywhere in the most diverse manifestations as the foundation of the objective world.

Here we stand at the point of departure for spiritual-scientific comprehension and perception of Christianity, and we begin to understand what a task and mission has been assigned to our movement for spiritual knowledge. In so doing, the reality of this mission becomes evident to us. Just as the individual human being has a physical, an etheric, and an astral body in addition to his or her ego, so it is with the historical development of Christianity, and both continue to rise to ever more lofty heights. We might say Christianity, too, has physical, etheric, and astral bodies, as well as an ego—an ego that can even deny its origin as it does in our time. To be sure, an ego can become egotistic, but it still remains an ego that can receive the true Christ Being into itself, thereby rising to ever higher stages of existence. What the human being is in particular, the great world is in its totality; and that includes its historical evolution.

If we look at the matter in this way, a perspective of the far-distant future opens itself before us from the spiritual-scientific point of view, and we know this perspective can touch our hearts and fill them with enthusiasm. More and more it becomes clear to us just what it is we have to do, and then we realize that we are not groping in the dark. This is so because we have not devised ideas that we intend to project into the future in an arbitrary fashion, but we intend to harbor and follow only those ideas that have been gradually prepared through centuries of Christian development. It is true that only after the physical, etheric, and astral bodies had come into existence could the ego make its appearance; now it is to be developed little by little to spirit self, life spirit, and spirit man. By the same token, modern human beings with their ego form and present thinking, could have developed only from the astral, etheric, and physical form of Christianity. Christianity has become ego. Just as truly as this was the development of the past, so it is equally true that the ego form of humanity can appear only after the astral and the etheric forms of Christianity have been developed. Christianity will develop on into the future. It will offer humanity far greater things, and the Christian development and way of life will arise in a new form. The transformed astral body will appear as the Christian spirit self, the transformed etheric body as the Christian life spirit. And in a radiant perspective of the future of Christianity, spirit man shines forth before our souls as the star toward which we strive, illuminated and glowing throughout with the spirit of Christianity.

Lecture III

More Intimate Aspects of Reincarnation

Munich, March 7, 1909

It is now my task to speak to the various groups about the more intimate aspects of reincarnation and various matters related to it because deep inside we must become more and more familiar with this subject matter and allow it to penetrate our being. In this context, we will also have to say a few things about the significance of the topic for the life of all humanity. Although we will also little by little discuss relevant questions of importance to the present age, we shall have to take very ancient times as our starting point. This is necessary because the method of inquiry in Spiritual Science differs from that employed by other theories of life or by the disciplines studying social problems. We in Spiritual Science treat the facts of life first in a general way, and then we elaborate on the details.

First of all, we express our world view in the most elementary sense through the statement that the human innermost core—an individual's divine ego—continues to develop from one life to another in successive incarnations. In the second instance, however, such a statement covers the question of reincarnation only in a very elementary way, and that is why we now want to speak about these things in greater detail and in a more intimate sense. Just saying that the ego of a human being hurries from one incarnation to another is not enough; there are many other phenomena connected with the subject of reincarnation, and only a discussion of how they are related to life itself will shed the right light on the issue. Let us begin to characterize reincarnation from this point of view by looking back into ancient times.

We have often talked about the fact that humanity must consider its ancestors to have come from ancient Atlantis, a former geographical region situated between what is today Africa and Europe on the one hand and America on the other. All the souls that are present today had already been incarnated in Atlantis, but in bodies that were in part considerably different from the ones we are accustomed to seeing. The Atlantean humanity had its own special form of leadership, and the soul-forces—indeed all the faculties—of the Atlanteans differed greatly from those of human beings. Hence, leadership as we know it today was nonexistent. In Atlantis, for example, there were no churches, ceremonial centers, or schools in the modern sense, but there existed an intermediate institution between ceremonial center and school; that is what we call the mystery sanctuaries or centers. Leadership of the Atlanteans with respect to learning and the conditions of external life was vested in these sanctuaries, and one could say that the spiritual leaders were at the same time kings of the Atlantean tribes. Initiates, whose mission can be circumscribed by a word of later coinage, by the word *oracle*, imported knowledge and exercised leadership in the mysteries. We therefore designate the great centers of Atlantean culture as the "Atlantean Oracles."

We have to get a clear understanding of the function of these oracles. They had to impart knowledge to human beings about the spiritual world behind the physical world. Knowledge such as this is different from ordinary knowledge in many ways; to stress only one difference, spiritual knowledge is not confined to space as is our present knowledge of the physical world. Anyone who, for example, knows about the mysteries of Mars also knows a great deal about

33

the spiritual mysteries of the entire universe. All the heavenly bodies of our solar system are interconnected, and as such they are the exterior expression of spiritual beings. The individual who knows these spiritual beings also knows the forces that are at work from one planet to another as well as in the spiritual world during the time between death and rebirth. And so it was the primary task of one oracle in Atlantis to transmit and proclaim to human beings the mysteries of Mars, whereas the primary task of another was to communicate the mysteries of Jupiter, and so on; and these compartmentalized insights made it possible to lead certain sections of the population. We shall speak about the reason for this at another occasion since our task today is a different one.

The Atlanteans were divided into groups, and part of the whole developmental process was that one group of human beings had to be governed especially by the forces that could be acquired through the knowledge of Mars. Other groups had to be governed by the forces acquired through the knowledge of Venus, or Mercury, and so on. In ancient Atlantis there were actually human beings alive whom we could call "Jupiter People" or "Mars People," and there were seven oracle centers because the populace in ancient Atlantis was divided into seven groups according to racial characteristics. The names applicable to these oracle centers corresponded to the names of the planets, but they were assigned to the oracles at a later time. The leadership of, and supreme sovereignty over, all other oracles was vested in what we may designate as the Atlantean Sun Oracle. Whatever oracles existed in the post-Atlantean periods—in Greece, Egypt, Asia, all were successors of the Sun Oracle in Atlantis. This is true also for the Apollo Oracle in Greece. The initiate who headed this Sun Oracle was the guardian of the deepest mysteries of our solar system. Together with his subordinates, he was called upon to investigate the nature of the spiritual life on the sun itself. His role was to proclaim to Atlantean humanity the secrets of the whole planetary system and to exercise supreme authority over the other oracle centers.

A very special task devolved on the Initiate of the Sun Oracle. It was to guide humanity in such a way that when the great catastrophe culminating in the submergence of Atlantis was over, the human race would be able to propagate and establish what we have often discussed as the post-Atlantean cultures. Specifically, the task of the Great Initiate of the Sun Oracle was to prepare human beings during the Atlantean time in such a way that they could enter the ancient Indian, Persian, Egypto-Babylonian-Hebraic, and Graeco-Roman cultures. To put it differently, the Great Initiate had to see to it that enough suitable soul material was available for these cultural epochs.

We must now inform ourselves a little about the task of this Great Initiate of the Sun Oracle. What were the essential features of Atlantean culture? Certainly it was quite different from later cultures. In ancient Atlantis, an individual belonging to the highest level of cultural life—the levels at which today's great leaders in, say, schoiarship, art, industry, or commerce can be found—was one who possessed extraordinary clairvoyant faculties and who was especially skilled in the use of magical powers. The qualities usually attributed to a leader or to a scholar were nonexistent in those days, or they were known only in the most primitive form. But although modern arithmetic, counting, logical reasoning, and intellectual deduction were unknown to the Atlanteans, they did possess primitive clairvoyant faculties and powers with which they could pierce into the spiritual worlds. Without the modern ego-consciousness, the Atlanteans saw into the spiritual world, and those whose vision was the most penetrating became the pillars of Atlantean culture. We have already stressed that the Atlanteans were able to manipulate certain inner forces of nature, for example the seed forces of plants; they propelled their vehicles with them, just as we utilize coal to propel our vehicles.

To repeat, the leaders of the Atlantean culture were not the people who tried, as the leaders of our time try, to unlock the secrets of the universe with their intellectual powers; rather, the leading individuals in Atlantis were those who excelled as clairvoyants and magicians. And those human beings who had the first rudimentary inkling about arithmetic, counting, logical reasoning, and intellectual deduction were in a certain sense despised because of their simplicity and were not considered as belonging to the aristocracy of cultural life. But it was precisely those human beings who possessed the very first rudimentary knowledge of the aforementioned skills and who were the most lacking in clairvoyant and magical powers whom the Great Leader of the Sun Oracle gathered from all regions. Yes, he assembled the most simple and, in a sense, the most despised people of ancient Atlantis—those who had first developed intellectual capacities. But those who were then at the highest level of cultural life and who were the acknowledged masters of a dimmed clairvoyance were not suitable material to be led through and beyond the great Atlantean catastrophe. No, the call of the Initiate went out to the simple people.

Incidentally, it may be said that we are living in an epoch today when a similar call is once again going out to humanity. To be sure, this appeal is what is appropriate for today, a time when humanity sees only what is in the physical world. The call to humanity issues from unknown depths of the spirit, depths that humanity will gradually become acquainted with, asking that humanity prepare itself for a new culture of the future, which will be permeated with clairvoyant powers. As with Atlantis, a catastrophe will occur, and afterwards a new culture imbued with spiritual capacities will arise, and it will be linked to what we call the idea of the universal brotherhood of humanity.

But today, as in Atlantean times, the call cannot go out to those who stand at the highest levels of cultural life because they will not understand. The Atlantean clairvoyants and magicians, who were in a way destined to die out with their culture, occupied a position similar to that of people in contemporary life who occupy the highest positions in the realms of scholarship and external industrial life—the great inventors and discoverers of our time. No matter how much the present leaders feel there is still to be done, they nevertheless occupy the same position as their Atlantean counterparts. Contemptuously they look down on those who are beginning to feel something of the spiritual life to come. The consciousness of this fact must be awakened in the soul of anyone whose cooperative efforts in the theosophical workshops are to be strengthened. When leading representatives of modern culture look contemptuously down at these small circles, those who are participating diligently in the preparation of future conditions must say to themselves that the intellectual giants of today cannot be counted on to lead the way in this task. It is precisely the people who are held in contempt because they are not considered to have reached the heights of contemporary erudition who are being assembled today, just as the leader of the Sun Oracle once gathered around him the simple of Atlantis. These disdained people are being assembled to prepare the dawn of a new culture whereas erudition of the modern form will bring about the twilight of our culture. This is mentioned in passing to fortify those who have to endure and hold their own against the attacks of the people who consider themselves to be on the cutting edge of contemporary culture.

The Great Initiate of the Sun Oracle gathered his simple

37

people in a region approximately to the west of present-day Ireland. Now we have to get a clear picture of the situation. It took Atlantis a long, long time to come to its end. Great masses of people were continually moving from the West toward the East. In the various regions of Asia, Europe, and Africa there were tribes who had arrived at different times and had intermingled. Then the Great Leader of the Sun Oracle took His small group of chosen people and made His way to Central Asia, where he established a colony from which the currents were to emanate that would later found the post-Atlantean cultures. However, in addition to His simple people, the Great Leader has taken something else with Him. And here we arrive at one of the chapters of human evolution, the truth of which we can comprehend only if we draw on the inner assurance gained by a steadfast engagement in Spiritual Science.

The Great Leader inspected, as it were, the other oracle centers for the purpose of finding in them the most notable initiates. Now there is a certain method by means of which "spiritual economy," as it may be called, can be put into practice. As you know, it is quite correct to say that the etheric body dissolves after a human being has died; what remains is an extract, and that is taken along. But the extract is only the elementary truth, which must be modified as one advances to higher levels of spiritual knowledge. It is not the case that the etheric bodies of all human beings are dissolved in the universal ether. Etheric bodies such as those possessed by the most notable initiates of the seven Atlantean Oracles are valuable. The spiritual achievements of these initiates were woven into their etheric bodies, and it would be against the principle of spiritual economy if the etheric bodies of the great initiates had simply been dissolved. They were to be preserved as prototypes for a later time, and it was incumbent upon the Great Initiate of the Sun Oracle to preserve the etheric bodies of the seven greatest ini-

38

tiates for this purpose. While leading His small group of simple people to Asia, He carried the etheric bodies of the seven most significant initiates of Atlantis with Him. Such a thing is possible through the methods that had been developed in the mystery centers. You have to visualize this as purely a spiritual process and not in the way as if one could wrap up etheric bodies and put them into boxes for safekeeping. What is certain, however, is that etheric bodies *can* be preserved for later times.

Over in Asia, the following happened. The simple people around the Leader propagated from one generation to another. Above all, these people had a tremendous devotion to and affection for their Great Leader. Their education was guided with wisdom and insight so that after many generations certain things occurred through one of the methods worked out in the mystery centers. Such methods are employed behind the scenes of external life, and we shall presently see how they take effect. Today's lecture will be the first in a series of several lectures designed to explain some of the details.

When a human being is descending to a new incarnation, he must envelop himself again with a new etheric body. Now, through the methods alluded to above, it is perfectly possible to weave into this new etheric body an old one that was preserved. And so after a diligent educational process, when the time had come, there were to emerge from the immigrants and their descendants seven individuals whose souls at their birth were sufficiently prepared to have the preserved etheric bodies of the seven greatest initiates of the Atlantean Oracles woven into their own etheric bodies. Thus, the preserved etheric body of the most important Saturn initiate was woven into that of one of the individuals gathered around the Great Leader of the Sun Oracle, the etheric body of the Mars initiate into another, the etheric body of the Jupiter initiate into a third, and so on. Hence the Great Leader of the Sun Oracle had seven individuals whose etheric bodies were interwoven with those of the most important initiates of the ancient Atlantean Oracles. If you had met these seven individuals somewhere in everyday life, you would have found them to be simple human beings, for they were not the reincarnated egos of the Atlantean initiates; they were merely simple human beings possessing the new faculties of the post-Atlantean era. Their egos were not much different from the egos of those who became the bearers of the first primitive and simple culture immediately after the Atlantean catastrophe. What made them different was that their etheric bodies contained the forces of the seven great Atlantean initiates, so we are dealing here not with a re-embodiment of the ego, but rather of the etheric bodies of these great initiates. Thus we see not only that the ego but also that the second member of the supersensible constitution—the etheric body—is capable of reincarnation. The seven individuals from among the followers of the Great Initiate of the Sun Oracle were inspired human beings simply by the fact that they had received these etheric bodies containing the forces and powers of the Atlantean era. At certain times their etheric bodies were capable of letting the forces stream into themselves that unveiled the mysteries of the Sun, Mars, Saturn, and so forth. Hence they appeared to be inspired individuals, but their utterances certainly exceeded anything their astral bodies or egos were able to understand.

What these seven inspired individuals taught from various parts of the world sounded like a wonderful harmonious choir, and after the seven had been united in the Lodge of the Seven Rishis, they were sent to India to inspire that country's ancient culture. Much that was profound in this culture has been preserved in a magnificent form in the Vedas,[27] and just as many wonderful ideas that give testimony to the deeply scientific nature of Indian culture have been preserved in the Upanishads,[28] in the Vedanta philosophy, and so on. However, the teachings of the ancient Holy Rishis, given in times when nothing was recorded, far exceed in beauty anything conveyed to us by the Indian scripts. What was written down in later times is at most a faint echo, for no records were kept of the primeval, sacred culture inspired by the Rishis; everything they taught was transmitted in a spiritual way through the mysteries.

We are interested today in learning how etheric bodies can be reincarnated, how the legacies of the ancient Atlantean epoch were transmitted by the Great Initiate of the Sun Oracle into the post-Atlantean era, and how they were then carried into the first culture of that era—into the resplendent Indian culture.

The mysteries of the Sun Oracle itself could not be directly revealed in ancient India, and that is why the seven Rishis spoke of a Being beyond their cognitive reach. They spoke of a Being who is the Leader of the Sun and directs its forces to the earth; they spoke of Vishva-Karman as a Being beyond the range of their knowledge. Vishva-Karman is none other than the Christ who was to appear later and whose coming had already been proclaimed in the ancient Indian culture.

The most important disciple of the Great Initiate of the Sun Oracle to receive the secrets of the Sun's essence was Zarathustra, who was subsequently to establish the second post-Atlantean culture. He was not the Zarathustra history talks about however. It was customary in ancient times that the successor of a great teacher or humanity took the name of his esteemed predecessor. No document contains any reference to the Zarathustra of whom we are now speaking; only his last successor is mentioned in history books. Yet it was the original Zarathustra who founded the primordial Persian culture and who was the first to point out to his Persian peoples that the sun not only possesses physical energy

41

but also spiritual power that streams down to earth. In his endeavor to awaken in his people a realization of this truth, Zarathustra's argument was as follows: If we direct our eyes to plants and everything else around us that contains life, we have to ask ourselves what we would be without sunlight. But together with the physical sunlight, a spiritual force also streams down to earth under the direction of a great sublime Being. Just as a human being has his or her physical body and an aura—we call it the small aura—so the sun has its physical body and its aura. Ahura Mazdao, the "great aura," consists of the group of great sun beings and their leader. Zarathustra spoke of this Ahura Mazdao, or Aura Mazdao—the Great Aura—and proclaimed the power of the sun aura by which the flow of evolution was made possible. However, Zarathustra also proclaimed that the forces of Ahriman would oppose the Sun Being. This then is what can be said about the external teachings of Zarathustra, but there is more to be said about him.

Zarathustra had some close disciples whom he initiated into the great mysteries of the world. We shall mention two of them in this context. To begin with the first, Zarathustra communicated to him all the wisdom necessary to bring about clairvoyance in the astral body, as well as the ability to perceive in one's present time frame simultaneously everything that is happening and all the mysteries spread out in both physical and spiritual space. To the second disciple Zarathustra transmitted what one might call the power to read the Akasha Chronicle, and this is nothing less than the clairvoyant power of the etheric body enabling the human being to perceive the successive phases of evolution in time. Thus, one disciple received the ability to perceive simultaneous events, and the other the vision of the Akasha Chronicle to perceive successive events that could lead to an understanding of the evolution of the earth and sun. By imparting these faculties to these disciples, Zarathustra had a profound effect on the continuation of culture in the post-Atlantean era.

The first disciple was reincarnated as the great individual who was to inspire and inaugurate the new currents of Egyptian culture, the being whom we know by the name of Hermes or Hermes Trismegistos. Through processes that are known, the astral body of Zarathustra was transmitted to Hermes so that he could proclaim the message of the higher worlds and their mysteries and incorporate them into Egyptian culture. Thus by processes we will gradually learn to understand, the astral body of Zarathustra was preserved and was transmitted to one disciple when he was born again as Hermes. Hermes wore Zarathustra's astral body as if it were a garment.

The other disciple was also reincarnated, and in him everything was meant to be revealed that is presented to the earth in the Akasha Chronicle. Since the etheric body of Zarathustra was to be woven into that of a disciple, a very special event had to take place to make this possible. The forces of the new etheric body somehow had to be illuminated in the disciple for his awakening. The Biblical story relates to us in a beautiful and marvelous way what this special event was. Allow your souls to visualize how it had to unfold.

You must first realize that this reborn disciple of Zarathustra possessed his own astral body and ego, and he was now to have the etheric body of Zarathustra woven into his soul. As a small child, he first had to feel how the forces of the etheric body of Zarathustra became active in him, and he had to feel this before the powers of judgment could be activated by his own astral body and before his own ego was able to interfere. So the special event that had to take place was some sort of initiation. The forces of Zarathustra's etheric body had to be awakened in this reborn disciple when he was a very small child, that is before his own individual development could come into play. For this reason, the child was placed into an ark of bulrushes that was then put into the water, so that he was completely cut off from the rest of the world and was unable to interact with it. That is when the forces of Zarathustra's etheric body that had been woven into him germinated and, as we said earlier, became illuminated.

I am sure you know by now that this reborn disciple of Zarathustra was none other than Moses. The Biblical story about his abandonment is really a presentation of that profound mystery behind the scenes of the external world dealing with the preservation of Zarathustra's etheric body and its reawakening in Moses. And this is how Hermes and Moses were able to guide the post-Atlantean culture through its recorded stages.

After hearing about these examples of the reincarnation of etheric bodies and of an astral body, we know it is insufficient to speak only of the reincarnation of the ego. Rather, the other members of the human constitution that we have become acquainted with—the etheric body and the astral body—can also be reincarnated. It is a principle of spiritual economy that what has once been gained cannot perish, but is preserved and transplanted on the spiritual soil of posterity. However, what we have described can be accomplished in another way. We shall see from an example that there are still other methods whereby the past is transported into the future.

You will remember a personality mentioned in the Bible: Shem, a son of Noah and progenitor of the Semitic people. Occult research confirms that there is an individual behind Shem that must be regarded as the tribal individuality of all Semitic peoples. When a number of human beings are to descend from a particular progenitor, a special provision must be made for this in the spiritual world. In the case of Shem, the provision was that an etheric body was specially

44

woven for him from the spiritual world, which he was to carry. This enabled him to bear in his own etheric body an especially exalted being from the spiritual world, a being who could not otherwise have incarnated on earth because it was incapable of descending into a compact physical body. This being was capable of incarnating only by virtue of the fact that it could now enter the etheric body of Shem. Since Shem had his own physical, etheric, and astral body, as well as his ego, he was first an individual in his own right. Beyond that, however, he was an individual whose etheric body was interwoven with the etheric body of another high being of the spiritual world, specially prepared for the purpose of founding a nation, as characterized above. If clairvoyant perception had confronted Shem, it would have seen Shem himself, but with a second entity extending out of him like a second being, yet still united with Shem's etheric body. This higher being was not Shem, but it incarnated in Shem—the human being—for a special mission. Unlike ordinary human beings, this higher being did not undergo various incarnations, but descended only once into a human body. Such a being is called an avatar. An avatar does not feel at home in the world as a human being would; he descends but once into this world for the sole purpose of carrying out a certain mission.

The part of a human being that is indwelled by such an avatar being acquires a special character in that it is able to multiply. When a grain of seed is sown into the ground, the stalk grows from it, and the grain is multiplied into the ears of grain. In the same way, the etheric body of Shem multiplied into many copies, and these were woven into all his descendants. That's what happened, and thus the copies of the etheric body that had been specially prepared in Shem as the prototype were woven into the etheric bodies of his direct descendants.

But this etheric body of Shem was later used in yet another

45

way. How this was done can best be placed before our souls by the visualization of an analogy. You may be a highly cultured European, but if you want to acquaint the Hottentots with your culture, you simply must learn their language. By analogy, the exalted beings that descend to earth to guide humanity must weave into themselves the forces by which they will be put into a position to communicate with human beings on earth. Now in the later phase of the evolution of the Semitic people, it became necessary that a very exalted being descend to earth in order to communicate with them and provide an impetus to their culture. Such a being was the Melchizedek of Biblical history who, as it were, had to "put on" the preserved etheric body of Shem—the very etheric body that was still inhabited by an avatar being. Once it was woven into him, Melchizedek was able to transmit to Abraham the impulse necessary for the continued progress of Semitic culture. Here, then, we have become acquainted with another unique way in which an etheric body develops in a particular human being and is subsequently allotted to a specially selected individuality for the fulfillment of a mission.

Such examples can be found up to the most recent times, and as we trace them, we gradually realize the truth of what occultism is able to say today about this subject matter. Occultism conveys to us that most human beings living at present no longer have etheric or astral bodies that were originally woven anew from the general fabric of the world. Almost every human being has in his or her etheric and astral body a fragment that has been preserved from ancient times because the principle of spiritual economy is at work preserving useful elements for repeated utilization.

Let us mention two more examples from the modern age that can illustrate to us how mysteries are at work from one epoch to another. The first example is related to the personality who is discussed in my book *Mysticism at the Dawn of the Modern Age:* Nicholas of Cusa. He called one of his writings *De docta ignorantia*, a Latin title that can be translated "Learned Ignorance"; yet it contains more erudition than many a book claiming to contain learned knowledge. There were certain reasons for the title. If you read other writings by Nicholas of Cusa, you will find that a prophetic presentation of the Copernican picture of the universe is woven into them in a curious way. Those who read carefully cannot fail to recognize it. Yet it was not until the time of Copernicus that the world was mature enough to accept this view of the universe in its actual form. Investigation into the connection reveals the following: One of the members of Cusa's supersensible constitution contained an ancient individuality of the highest rank, and that made it possible for the astral body of Nicholas of Cusa to be preserved and then to be woven into the astral body of Nicholas Copernicus. The wisdom once possessed by Nicholas of Cusa could, as it were, be resurrected in Copernicus, and that is an example of how the astral body has reincarnated.

The second example deals with Galileo, who has been immensely important for modern thought, as many of you who have thought about the matter know. Without him, there would have been no physics in the modern sense because the whole mode of thinking in terms of physics today must be attributed to Galileo. Every schoolboy today will read in the most elementary books of Galileo's law of inertia, of continuity, which indicates that a body in motion tends to continue its movement until it encounters an obstacle. Thus, if we throw some object, it will travel forward by its own momentum until it is stopped by an obstacle or outer force. This is how we think today, and this is what children in school learn from their textbooks. However, people living before Galileo thought in a different manner. They thought that if a stone were thrown, its flight could not continue unless the air drove or pushed it from behind. So we see that

47

the laws of falling bodies, of the pendulum, and of simple machines are all derived from Galileo.

Galileo received his insights through a certain inspiration. I need only to remind you of how he discovered the law of the pendulum by observing the swinging lamp in the Cathedral at Pisa—a stroke of genius. Many people had walked past this lamp without noticing a thing, but when Galileo observed it, the fundamental laws of mechanics dawned on him. A human being who can be inspired in such a profound way has an etheric body of enormous richness; to allow it to perish would contradict the law of spiritual economy.

It is for this reason that Galileo's etheric body too was preserved and reappeared after a comparatively short period of time in an individual whose achievements were also to be of great significance. It was woven into a personality who grew up in a remote peasant village in Russia, ran away from his parents, and journeyed to Moscow. The great talent of this young man became apparent very soon, and he rapidly absorbed the knowledge of his day in the schools of Russia and Germany, so that he had soon encompassed the total of the general knowledge available in the culture of his time. All he had to do was to accumulate the knowledge developed on earth since he had died—in his etheric body—as Galileo. And then this very same person became, so to speak, the founder of the whole classical literature movement in Russia, creating lasting literary treasures practically out of the void. But more than that, he also provided important stimuli to every scientific discipline related to physics and chemistry, and particularly to all areas of mechanics. This individual was none other than Michail Lomonosov, whose achievements and reforms were possible only because the etheric body of Galileo had been woven into him. Galileo died in the middle of the seventeenth century, and Michail Lomonosov was born early in the eighteenth century with Galileo's etheric body, representing one of those intimate reincarnations where a member of the supersensible constitution of the human being other than the ego is reincarnated. Such things lead us toward a deep understanding of the entire evolutionary process and of many other factors that have developed in the course of time, leading to the conditions prevailing at present.

The greatest avatar on earth was Christ Himself, who lived for three years in the three bodies of Jesus of Nazareth. Because Christ lived in the three bodies of the supersensible constitution of Jesus of Nazareth, it was possible for the latter's etheric and astral bodies, and of the ego too in a lesser degree, to multiply in the same way as we have discussed it before. After the Mystery of Golgotha and as a result of the wonderful laws of spiritual economy, quite a few copies of the astral body and of the etheric body of Jesus of Nazareth were present as archetypes in the spiritual world. If an avatar enters a human sheath, the essence of the host is dispersed into many replicas. In contrast to the copies of Shem's etheric body, the copies of the astral and etheric bodies of Jesus of Nazareth had another special characteristic. The copies of Shem's etheric body could be implanted only into his own descendants whereas the copies of the etheric body and the astral body of Jesus of Nazareth could be implanted into all human beings of the most diverse peoples and races. A copy of the archetypal astral and etheric bodies of Jesus of Nazareth could be implanted in anyone who through his or her personal development had become ready for this transfer, no matter what race such an individual belonged to. And we see how in this subsequent evolution of Christendom, strange developments take place behind the external historical façade, and only such developments can render the external course of events intelligible.

Now, how did Christianity spread? We can say that in the first few centuries the dissemination of the idea of Christianity depended on what happened on the physical plane. In this era we see that Christianity is decidedly propagated through everything that lives on the physical plane. The Apostles stressed the fact that the propagation of Christianity was based on direct physical perception of eyewitnesses. "We have laid our hands into His wounds" was a statement of proof that the Christ had walked on earth in a human body. In other words, the stress was put on anything on the physical plane that could serve as documentation for the development of Christianity. Time and again during those first few centuries, it was asserted that those who had been disciples of the Apostles themselves were responsible for the continuing propagation of Christianity, and it was emphasized that they had known the immediate followers of the Lord Himself. So we see that people in this era relied, as it were, on eyewitness reports, and this continues in a still deeper sense up to the time of St. Augustine, who said: "I would not believe in the truth of the Gospels if the authority of the Catholic Church did not compel me to do so." Why, then, did he believe? Because it was his conviction that the visible Church has propagated the Gospel on the physical plane from one decade and from one century to another. However, in the following centuries, from the fifth to the tenth, Christianity was propagated in a different way. Why and how? It is instructive to learn the answer to this question if we are interested in following the spiritual progress of human evolution.

You can visualize the method of propagation in this next period by considering, for example, the Old Saxon gospel epic entitled *Heliand*. In this work, a kind of initiate presents his readers with his version of the Christ idea and with his perception of the Christ-Being. The Heliand, the Savior, presented by this Saxon initiate is a supersensible being. Yet, He is portrayed not within the context of the events in Palestine, but rather as a prince of a Germanic tribe. The disciples are individuals from Germanic lands, and the whole of Christianity is clothed in Central European imagery. Why was this done? It was done because the initiate who wrote the *Heliand* at the suggestion of Louis the Pious had clairvoyant faculties, so that he was able to see Christ in a way similar to Paul's perception of Christ at Damascus. Through the event at Golgotha the Christ-Being had united Himself with the astral body of the earth, thereby infusing His power into the aura of the earth; and when Paul became clairvoyant, he could clearly perceive: The Christ *is* present! Paul did not allow himself to become a believer merely on the strength of what was reported to have happened in Palestine. Only after he had seen the being that was woven into the earth with his own eyes did he change from Saul to Paul. In a similar vision, the Risen Christ, the eternal Christ living in the spiritual world after Golgotha, was revealed to the writer of the *Heliand*, and He was more important to him than was the historical Christ of Palestine. And so he presents Him in another setting because the spiritual Christ was more important to him than was the external image of the Christ. You may want to ask why the author of the *Heliand* was able to communicate such an image from clairvoyant perception. He was able to do this because a copy of the etheric body of Jesus of Nazareth was woven into his own etheric body. This was the case because during these centuries—starting with the fifth or sixth and ending with the ninth or tenth century—the etheric bodies of those who were destined to do something for the advancement of Christianity were interwoven with a copy of the etheric body of Jesus of Nazareth, and one of these special individuals was the writer of the *Heliand.*

Since there were many others who had a copy of the etheric body of Jesus of Nazareth woven into their own etheric body, we can readily see that human beings in these centuries lived in imaginations that were closely related to

51

the events in Golgotha. All those who created the original artistic portrayals of the Savior on the cross and of Mary with the Jesus Child had been inspired to do pictorial representations of anything connected with the event in Golgotha by one and the same thing: a copy of the etheric body of Jesus of Nazareth was woven into the etheric body of each of these individuals. If the paintings of the events in Golgotha seemed like representations of a type, this points to the fact that all the artists were clairvoyant; what they created was then transmitted to posterity by the forces of tradition. In these early centuries, not all the inspired individuals destined to propagate the idea of Christianity were, of course, artists. Take, for example, John Scotus Erigena,[29] the scholastic philosopher, who in the days of Charles the Bald wrote the famous *De Divisione Naturae.* He, too, had a copy of the etheric body of Jesus woven into his own etheric body.

If human beings were born during the period from the fifth to the tenth centuries who had a copy of the etheric body of Jesus of Nazareth woven into their own etheric bodies, human beings living in the period from the eleventh to the fifteenth centuries received copies of the astral body of Jesus of Nazareth rather than copies of His etheric body. Only by considering this fact do we fully understand some of the important personalities of that time. How will a personality whose own astral body is interwoven with a copy of the astral body of Jesus appear to the outside world? After all, the ego of Jesus is not incarnated in such an individual; each personality retains his or her own ego. Ego judgment can cause many an error to creep into the life of such an individual; but because the copy of the great prototype has been woven into his or her astral body, devotion, all the feelings, everything in short that permeates and weaves through this astral body will come to the fore as the intrinsic essence of the astral body, even though it may perhaps be at variance with the ego itself. Think of Francis of Assisi.

There you have a personality into whose astral body a copy of the astral body of Jesus of Nazareth was woven. You may have found many extremes in the biography of Francis of Assisi, and if you did, you should consider that they were caused by his ego, which was not on the same level with his astral body. But the moment you study his soul under the assumption that his ego was not always capable of making the right judgments about the wonderful feelings and the humility contained in the astral body, then you will understand him. A copy of the astral body of Jesus of Nazareth was reincarnated in Francis of Assisi, and this was the case with many individuals of that time—Franciscans, Dominicans, and all other personalities of that time who will be intelligible only when studied in the light of this knowledge. For example, one of those personalities was the renowned St. Elisabeth of Thüringen.

And so what has happened in the external life of our existence becomes fully intelligible only when we see how spiritual impulses are conveyed in each era and how they are propagated in the course of time.

When Christ incarnated in Jesus of Nazareth, something like an imprint of the ego was made in the astral body of Jesus of Nazareth. When the Christ-Being entered the astral body, we can easily conceive that something like a replica of the ego could be produced in the surrounding parts of the astral body. This copy of the ego of Christ Jesus produced many duplicates that were preserved, so to speak, in the spiritual world. In the case of a few individuals who were to be prophets for their own age, something was woven into their ego. Among them were the German mystics who proclaimed the inner Christ with such fervor because something like a copy of the ego of Christ was incarnated in them—only a copy or image of Christ's ego, of course. Only human beings who prepare themselves gradually for a full understanding of the Christ and who understand through their knowledge of the spiritual worlds what the Christ really *is*, as He surfaces time and again in ever changing forms during the course of human evolution—only those human beings will also gradually gain the maturity necessary to experience Christ in themselves. They will be ready to absorb, so to speak, the waiting replicas of the Christ-Ego, ready to absorb the ego that the Christ imprinted in the body of Jesus.

Part of the inner mission of the universal stream of spirituality is to prepare human beings to become so mature in soul that an ever-increasing number of them will be able to absorb a copy of the Ego-Being of Christ Jesus. For this is the course of Christian evolution: first, propagation on the physical plane, then through etheric bodies, and then through astral bodies that, by and large, were reincarnated astral bodies of Jesus. Now the time is at hand when the ego-nature of Christ Jesus will increasingly light up in human beings as the innermost essence of their souls. Yes, these imprinted copies of the Christ Jesus individuality are waiting to be taken in by human souls—they are waiting!

And now you see from what depths the universal stream of Spiritual Science flows into our souls. Spiritual Science is not a theory, not the sum total of concepts given merely for the intellectual enlightenment of human beings; it is a reality, and it intends to offer realities to the human soul. Those who wish to gain a spiritual understanding of Christianity and experience it within themselves will strive to make a personal contribution so that either in the present or in a later incarnation a copy of the Christ Jesus individuality can be woven into their own egos. A person who understands the true, inmost essence—the actuality—of the universal stream of Spiritual Science will prepare himself or herself not just for knowledge, but rather for an encounter with actual reality. You must develop a feeling that we in our world movement are not concerned with the mere communication of theories, but rather with preparing human beings to accept facts. We are also concerned that human beings receive what is waiting in the spiritual world and what they have the power to receive, provided they prepare themselves for this task in the right way.

Lecture IV

Results of Spiritual Scientific Investigations of the Evolution of Humanity: I

Rome, March 28, 1909

Tonight we will talk about sin, original sin, illness, and so on. Let us first look backwards into the past and then allow the future to pass by our spiritual eyes. We have before our modern era the time of Rome and Athens, which was preceded by the Egyptian-Chaldaic period; actual historical records are lacking for the time before then. However, for these older prehistorical epochs there are two sources that can give information; ancient religious teachings for those who know how to decipher them and retrospective images that can be perceived by clairvoyant consciousness. It is the latter we wish to discuss.

Everything on earth is subject to the laws of evolution, and that is especially true for the life of the human soul. The life of the soul in ancient times was different from what it is today. In prehistoric times, thousands of years in the past, the scope of the souls of human beings in Europe, Asia, and Africa was much wider and more comprehensive than that of human beings of our time. To be sure, they did not have the kind of mind that enables us to read or to do arithmetic, but they did possess a primitive clairvoyance and a tremendous memory of which ours cannot have the slightest notion. We shall see later why that was so.

To give you an idea of how these prehistoric people perceived the world, let me tell you, for example, that they saw everything surrounded by an aura when they awakened to their day-consciousness. A flower, for instance, appeared to them surrounded by a circle of light similar to that we see around the light of street lamps in the evening fog. And during sleep these human beings were able to perceive the soul-spiritual beings in their full reality. Human beings learned gradually to see the contours of objects more clearly, but simultaneously and in direct proportion to their ability to do so, the conscious interaction with the spiritual world and the beings in it decreased; it ceased altogether when the ego became individualized in every single being.

The earth, too, had quite a different configuration in those early ages. Human beings lived in other regions and on other continents, and our own ancestors lived on a continent that is now covered by the Atlantic Ocean. The traditional name for this continent is Atlantis, and its disappearance as well as the legend of the universal flood is related in the myths of all peoples. The Atlantean culture was magnificent, and mankind lost many important insights with its destruction, insights that now can be retrieved only with great difficulty. Just as we in our times know how to harness the forces hidden in fossil plants—coal—for trade and industry, so the ancient Atlanteans knew how to utilize the driving forces in grain as energy, for example for the purpose of propelling their air vehicles that moved just a little bit above the ground in air that was much denser than is ours.

Let us now look at the physical organism of the Atlantean individual. It had the peculiar characteristic that the etheric body was not completely identical with the physical body and that the head of the etheric body projected beyond the head of the physical body. This peculiarity is connected with the clairvoyant capabilities of the Atlanteans, also with their extraordinary memory and with their magical powers. The ether-head had a special and central point of perception.

57

When the ether-head in the course of evolution retracted more and more into the physical head, the profile was changed. Now we have at that point an organ, the development of which will restore the power of clairvoyance in humanity: the pineal gland. And thus, the clairvoyant power of the Atlanteans, as well as their tremendous memory and their magical powers, disappeared gradually; and in its place we developed our present ability to think and to do mathematics.

Going still farther back, we find other catastrophes. The volcanos that we have today are the last remnants of an epoch when whole parts of the earth were destroyed by fire. The continent that perished in those times is designated by the name "Lemuria" and was the area that is now largely taken up by the Pacific and Indian Oceans. The inhabitants of that continent had bodies that were quite different from human bodies in our age and by our standards would appear grotesque. The relationship of the physical to the astral body was different in those early human beings. The crown of the head was open, and rays of light penetrated this opening, so that the head was surrounded by a resplendent aura, and this gave one the appearance of having a lantern on top. The last remnant of this Lemurian head structure can be seen today when we look at the head of a newborn baby and discover the small opening on top that remains open for about a year or a little longer. The bodies of the Lemurians had gigantic dimensions and were made out of a fine, almost gelatine-like substance.

Human beings in the Lemurian age were not at all independent and could do only the things they were inspired to do by the spiritual forces within whom they were, in a manner of speaking, imbedded. Receiving everything from these forces, they acted as if driven by a soul-instinct. At this time the powerful effect of spiritual beings who had not descended into a physical incarnation made itself felt. These

58

beings, who were not well-disposed to humanity, had such an effect on humanity that it attained the independence it had lacked heretofore. According to divine providence, mankind was certainly meant to attain this independence some day, but only through the influence of these beings did that independence come about so early. Together with the other forces, these beings slipped into the astral bodies of human beings, who had not yet entered into a close relationship with their own essence, and bestowed on them a kind of will power that would enable them to do evil since it was only astral and not guided by reason. The influence of these forces, called Luciferic forces, as we can see, may be good or bad because, on the one hand, they led mankind astray and, on the other, gave it freedom.

Today's consciousness originated in clairvoyant consciousness, which we find increasingly more developed as we go back in human evolution. The Lemurians were able to perceive things only with their soul. They were, for example, unable to perceive the form, the color, or the external qualities of a flower. It revealed itself to them as a shining astral configuration that they perceived with a kind of inner organ. According to the divine plan, human beings were not supposed to perceive the world with external sense organs before the middle of the Atlantean period, but the Luciferic forces made this happen earlier, at a time when human instincts had not yet matured. That represents the "Fall" of mankind. Religious documents tell us that the snake opened man's eyes, but without the interference of Lucifer the human body would not have become as firm as it now is and the Atlantean humanity would have been able to see the spiritual side of all things. Instead, man fell into sin, illusion, and error, and to make things worse, toward the middle of the Atlantean period he was also subjected to the influence of Ahrimanic forces. The Luciferic forces had worked on the astral body, but the Ahrimanic forces worked on the etheric body, especially on the ether-head. By that, many human beings fell into the error of mistaking the physical world for the world of truth. The name "Ahrimanic" comes from Ahriman, the name the Persians gave to this erroneous principle. Zoroaster told his people about Ahriman, warned them about him, and exhorted them to become one with Ahura Mazdao—Ormuzd. Ahriman is identical with Mephistopheles and has nothing to do with Lucifer. Mephistopheles comes from the Hebrew word *me-phis-to-pel*, which means the liar, the cheater. Satan in the Bible is Ahriman too, not Lucifer.

Ancient Atlantis was gradually destroyed in the course of centuries by floods, and the inhabitants left over from the catastrophe retreated to regions that had been spared, such as Asia, Africa, and America. The first region in which Atlantean culture continued to develop was the area that later came to be called India. There the people kept a clear memory of the earlier clairvoyance and of the perception of the spiritual world. It was therefore not difficult for their teachers—the Rishis—to direct their attention to the spiritual side of the world, and initiation was easy to achieve. Clairvoyance was never completely lost; there always existed some clairvoyant people up to the time of Christ. We can recognize a remnant of this primitive form of clairvoyance in mythology, in which the central concern was with beings who had actually been alive, such as Zeus, Apollo, and so forth. Although the Ahrimanic influence began in the Atlantean epoch, as we have said, it unfolded its full strength only later in human evolution. The ancient Indians were sufficiently protected against Ahriman; for them the physical world was never anything else but *maya*, illusion. Only in the most ancient Persian period of Zarathustra did people begin to place value on the physical world and thereby come into the power of Ahriman. This clarifies for us Zarathustra's admonition of which we spoke earlier.

As the evolution of humanity reached the Greek period, human beings were confronted by another force that began to drive them back up to the spiritual world from which, as it were, they had been expelled since the Lemurian age. This new force was the Christ-Principle, which entered Jesus of Nazareth and permeated His three bodies—the physical, the etheric, and the astral. When the human soul is completely imbued with the Christ-Principle, the Ahrimanic and Luciferic powers will be defeated, and through this principle the course of evolution will be reversed. Christ would not have been able to influence humanity had His coming not been announced to it a long time before He actually appeared. Inwardly, however, humanity has always been led by Christ; we can deduce this from the magnificent images by which His coming was prophesied. Who else could have inspired such mighty imaginations?

Immediately after the mystery of Golgotha when Christ's blood ran from five wounds and His spirit permeated the lowest realms, the incarnation of Christ brought about a remarkable change in the physical, etheric, and astral bodies of humanity. Christ's etheric and astral bodies multiplied like a grain of seed, and the spiritual world was filled with these copies. For example, human beings living in the period from the fifth or sixth through the tenth centuries who had developed sufficiently received at their birth such an imprint of the Christ-Incarnation of Jesus of Nazareth. St. Augustine is the individual in whom such partaking in the etheric body of Christ is most clearly evident, and the great significance of his life must be attributed to this fact. On the other hand, Christ's astral body was incorporated into human beings from about the tenth to the sixteenth centuries, and this explains the appearance of human beings who were endowed with extraordinary humility and virtue, such as St. Francis of Assisi and the great Dominicans who reflected the wonderful astral qualities of Christ. These individuals were imbued with such a clear image of the great truths they practiced throughout their lives. By contrast, St. Augustine was never free of doubt and always experienced the conflict between theory and practice. Of the great Dominicans, St. Thomas Aquinas[30] is especially noteworthy because in him the influence of the astral body of Christ was manifest to a high degree, as we shall see later. Beginning with the sixteenth century, copies of the Christ-Ego begin to weave themselves into the egos of a few individualities, one of them being Christian Rosenkreutz,[31] the first Rosicrucian. This phenomenon led to the feasibility of a more intimate relationship with Christ, as is revealed by esoteric teaching.

The power of Christ will make human beings more perfect, spiritualize them, and lead them back into the spiritual world. Mankind developed its reason at the expense of clairvoyance; the power of Christ will enable human beings to learn on this earth and to ascend again with what they will have acquired on earth. Human beings descended from the Father, and the power of Christ will lead them back to the Father.

Lecture V

Results of Spiritual Scientific Investigations
of the Evolution of Humanity: II

Rome, March 31, 1909

What happened at Golgotha as a germinal event has
undergone a slow and gradual development. This mystery
built the bridge from the past to the future because the soul
life of humanity underwent a profound metamorphosis.
This becomes especially clear when one looks at two great
individuals who prepared the way for Christianity: St.
Augustine and St. Thomas Aquinas. To understand these
two men properly, it will be necessary to look at the old
mystery centers where the highest knowledge was taught.
Not to do this would make it impossible to gain a thorough
understanding of these personalities.

As we know, all nations or peoples in the past had the so-
called mystery centers. Here we shall point out only their
most basic features and refer to them henceforth as "Mysteries." First of all, these were institutions in which the
church and school were subsumed. They taught first of all
the origin of creation and its continuation, but their teaching
was not a dull doctrine like the modern doctrine of creation,
but rather a body of knowledge that culminated in clairvoyant
perception. In the true Mysteries there was no separation
between belief and knowledge. They were divided into higher
and lower Mysteries, with the latter describing the evolution of the earth in magnificent images, so that everything

was permeated by art and beauty. Art, religion, and knowledge all derived from the same source.

The individual who wanted to advance further was given elementary and general exercises. What today we call theosophical knowledge was then only a preparation. This was followed by exercises similar to the ones we have described in recent lectures, although they were conducted in a different manner and were not Christian or Rosicrucian in nature. This is how the astral body was organized for many years. Then the following happened, something that is no longer necessary today because of changed conditions: When the hierophant saw that the astral body of the person to be initiated had matured sufficiently, a death-like state was induced in the subject for a period of three and a half days so that the body was similar to that of Lazarus. This was also the occasion when the etheric body, together with the other two higher bodies, was almost completely removed from the physical body. The disciple during these three and a half days had a vision of the spiritual world and experienced a state of illumination that enabled him to reach into the highest regions and perceive everything that is related to past and future. After the three and a half days, the disciple was awakened and was then able to relate what was happening in the higher spheres. He had been able to see that Christ, the leading Spirit in our evolution, would be lying in the grave for three and a half days. It is this fact that makes the Mysteries historical reality.

The Mystery of Golgotha was the culmination of what was happening in the lower Mysteries because earlier presentiments became fact in it. Whereas the "I" of the disciple had earlier been successful in changing the astral body through exercises of the imagination, the Mystery of Golgotha brought about a metamorphosis of the etheric body. Whatever was changed in the astral body became *manas*, or spirit self—the actual spirit, the higher "I." On the other hand, whatever part of the etheric body was changed constituted *buddhi*, or life spirit. Then the disciple could also try to change his physical body, and this resulted in *atma: Atmung*,[32] so called because in reality the transformation of the physical body was attained through special breathing exercises. Only through the formation of *buddhi* can the human being recognize and perceive Christ as spiritual essence.

Why was it necessary to remove the astral body first? Had the astral body continued to be tied to the physical body, it would not have had the strength to imprint certain impressions onto the ether body. The Christ has liberated us from this three and a half day test, and it is through Him that the exercises mentioned above have become possible without intercession by the hierophant. We see the first example of this in Saul when he became Paul. What happened to him on his way to Damascus must be interpreted as something similar to an initiation. The reason that he needed only a few minutes for it was that he had attained a certain maturity in the preceding life. The line between the connecting point in the present life and the one in the previous incarnation, in which a certain learning experience took place, may be interrupted by several intermediate incarnations, and it is also possible for such a previous learning experience not to surface until late in the present life. This explains why the conversion of Saul, that is his connecting himself with his previous development, took place at a relatively mature age. In addition, Paul did not have to project himself into higher worlds in order to perceive the Christ, as would have been necessary for other initiates of the pre-Christian era. After all, Christ did remain on earth as He was intimately united with its astral body. Had a clairvoyant observer perceived the events from another star, he would have been able to see the tremendous transformation that the Mystery of Golgotha had brought about.

To gain knowledge in ancient times, everything had to

be learned and understood in the Mysteries, but things are different in more modern times, as the lives of St. Augustine and Thomas of Aquinas prove. Before these men lived, it would have been futile to talk about the spiritual hierarchies because one who was not initiated was not able to perceive them. We can attribute this inability to gaze into the spiritual world to the fact that the Mysteries had ceased to exist six hundred years before Christ, and initiations no longer took place after that. The schools of philosophy took the place of the genuine Mysteries, and philosophy itself took the place of the initiation. However, philosophy was not always as abstract a system as it is today; on the contrary, especially in the beginning it was more or less completely reminiscent of the Mysteries. Aristotle[33] was the last from whom we have such a philosophy, but the resonance of the Mysteries was already reduced to a bare minimum in his philosophy. After Aristotle, things went so far as to make people forget that every philosophy must be traced back to the wisdom of the Mysteries. What came later is only an infiltration of abstract terms, similar to the construction of a thatched roof.

The first step forward is characterized by the Mystery of Golgotha. Up to this time the human faculties, for example reason, were little developed. Human beings could not make any progress because their minds were bound to their sense organs, and the time when the mind could develop independently was not yet at hand. What happened at Golgotha could not be grasped just by using one's mind. However, when Christ left the material world, innumerable copies of His etheric and astral body came into being; these were destined to be woven into the bodies of human beings suited to disseminate Christianity. One of them was Augustine, who descended to the physical plane for a new incarnation and wanted to form a new etheric body for himself. It was then that one of the copies of the etheric body of Christ

66

was woven into his own etheric body, and this is how it became possible for him to find in himself the sources of his doctrine about the true form of Christian mysticism. But because he had received only the etheric body of Christ, his ego was subjected to error, and it was possible for him to succumb to his passions. And this is how Augustine developed his ego, but also committed errors and went through all stages of doubt in regard to Christ's teaching. What we see in him is a sort of higher materialism because even in those days people fell into the mistake of wanting to materialize everything. Only the person who frees himself or herself from this tendency will understand spiritual things. When Augustine finally found the spirit of Christianity in the words of John and Paul, the etheric body of Christ began to work in him, for he speaks not of the physical body but of the etheric body, which is the same as what he calls "soma." In speaking of the "sense," he refers to the astral body, and he says of the ego that it can rise in him through purification. The transformation of the astral body he calls "laying hold of the truth," and that of the etheric body he delineates as "being joyful and enjoying spiritual things." Finally, his term for the highest degree of spiritualization is "the vision." The writings of Augustine are a good preparation for us because they present the inner development of a mystic. One can clearly recognize the moment in which he enters the spiritual world. Augustine is the best interpreter of Paul's letters.

Now let us look at another great representative of Christianity: Thomas Aquinas. Comparing him with Augustine, we see that he was not caught up in the errors of Augustine and that, beginning with his childhood years, he did not experience doubt or lack of faith. This is not surprising because judgment and conviction reside in the astral body, and Christ's astral body was woven into his own. The implantation of any principle into the human body can take place only when an external event changes the natural course of things. When Thomas was still a child, lightning struck nearby and killed his little sister. This seemingly purely physical event made him suitable to receive into his own astral body that of Christ.

Thomism coincides with the time when the human mind as we know it began to develop. The strongest impulse of this formative process came from Arabism, a truly intellectual science. Whereas before the old sages knew why they were able to gaze directly into the spiritual world, the new philosophy could make good use of Aristotle because he was one of the first great thinkers who preferred intellectual work to the wisdom of the Mysteries. The latter disappeared complete with the purely intellectual speculation of Arabism. Such speculation could at best culminate in a pantheism of rational concepts, but it could not conceive of more than this idea of a unified whole. Now, Thomas adopted the intellectual science accessible to him, but he left revealed knowledge intact and made use of dialectics in order to understand it.

The New Testament contains everything of revealed knowledge, so that Thomas had only to add the finely polished science to the explanations. Scholasticism, which is not much appreciated these days, made this intellectual science possible; but by using progressive dialectics, Thomas also made it possible for human beings to elevate themselves again to the divine idea. Scholasticism comes from the Greek *scole* and therefore means "paying attention," but was erroneously translated as *scuola*, school. The scholastic system was the most perfect web of logic, and it enabled Thomas to think anew the pre-creational divine thoughts, freed from error and delusion as they can be conceived of only in monastic seclusion far away from the noise of the world.

Human beings are eager to comprehend quickly, to adopt an idea and make it their own, and to simplify everything.

But the divine is not that simple! With Thomas Aquinas, human thought rises to new heights. Being no less a mystic than a scholastic, Thomas was able to give us such vivid descriptions, similar to those of the seer Dionysius the Areopagite[34] because he saw the spiritual hierarchies and thus he was able to solve the most difficult problems during his long nightly meditations in front of the altar. Therefore, we find combined in him the qualities of the mystic and of a brilliant thinker who is not influenced by the senses. No important concepts were added after him, not even the term "evolution," which, by the way, can already be found in Aristotle's writings and is perhaps even better described there.

We have already stated before that the New Testament contains everything. Specifically, it also contains the seed of mysticism, and we have seen how this seed has ripened and how an infinite number of treasures have been unearthed from the Gospels. Nowadays, we have theosophy; later there will be other spiritual waves, and new treasures will be found in the Gospels. The revelation of John concludes the future of the earth.

Today I have tried to show you how the liberation of the intellect was the first stage of Christianity. This is only one leaf, but others will grow on the mighty plant of Christianity, one after the other. The blossom will be the total beauty of the earth, renewed through Christianity, and the fruit will be the new world for which today's earth is the preparation.

As Christ taught, is still teaching, and will be teaching to the end, He can be found by those who seek Him.

Lecture VI

On the Occasion of the Dedication of the
Francis of Assisi Branch

Malsch, April 6, 1909

Today we are gathered for the dedication ceremony of
our anthroposophical branch in Malsch. Although this
"Section" of our Society has been fully at work for a while,
we are able only today to officially celebrate its opening.

Many of our anthroposophical friends have come to this
celebration from the most diverse regions to which our anthroposophical endeavors have spread. By coming here, they
have demonstrated that they wish to unite their anthroposophical feelings and thoughts with those of serious and hard-
working people in this group. One might say this group of
people in Malsch has been thrown into these remote moun-
tains, but surrounded by all the beautiful, great, and noble
forces of nature, they will successfully unfold anthroposophical life. Those of you who were able to look around in the
vicinity of this hospitable house in Malsch will have noticed
that much has been done for its external appearance, as if
the people responsible wished to say externally that the
spiritual life by which all of us are inspired shall find special
expression in this beautiful spot.

Let us look back at the modest beginnings of our anthroposophical life at the founding of our German Section, into
which the Section in Malsch is now being incorporated. At
that time we began with but a small group of people of spir-

itual scientific enthusiasts. Then, as we look at events such as this one today and observe the large number of souls who unite with us in spiritual scientific feelings and sentiments, we can be satisfied with the last few years of our endeavors.

The Stockmeyer family has spared no efforts to help with the unfolding of spiritual life on this beautiful piece of land although the spirits of nature have clearly aided their efforts. Also, this family must find great satisfaction in seeing how many genuine and true friends have hurried to this hospitable place, and I am sure all anthroposophical friends may be justly called genuine and true friends. This is so because anthroposophy must above all be truth in our hearts, and truth is sincerity. Anthroposophy, therefore, must be sincere; and anthroposophical friendship is expressed by your participation in such a dedication festival. Everything must be imbued with sincerity because honesty in friendship unites us with those who have worked so industriously so that here, too, there would arise a working sphere of anthroposophic activity. The hearts of those who have come here will be filled with gratitude for the efforts of the Stockmeyer family, who can be assured of our truly sincere anthroposophical appreciation.

On the other hand, the very success of such a dedication festival with so many souls present shows that Spiritual Science in our time is a powerful magnet for human striving, and on this occasion it may also be fitting to say that we can certainly look beyond the rooms that, surrounded by the spirits of beautiful nature, enclose us today and look at the rest of the world. It is possible to say that life and the endeavors of Spiritual Science today appear as phenomena whose existence results from an inner necessity. Really, it is as if many a page in the book about the life of old cultures, which sustained European and Western humanity for millennia and gave security and strength for life to it, were now beginning to wither and appear cold and lifeless to human hearts. That is why we see today a longing for spiritual scientific truths in so many areas of life. I, for one, having been permitted to speak to you here, sense something like a future force at work because of what has been taking place around me in the last few days.

We are here surrounded by green trees, the budding life of nature, and also by the magnificent sunlight that shines on us benevolently at this dedication since it animates everything and is imbued with spirit. This, then, is a perfect place to relate to you the words of our great harbingers of the new wisdom, the Masters of Wisdom and of the Harmony of Feelings.

A few days have passed since I was permitted to speak in the same spirit in a lecture cycle in Rome, and this event symbolized to me what a magnet spiritual striving is. I was to speak to those who harbor a spiritual scientific longing in their hearts, but their longing is still fairly undefined at times. Yet the place where I was to speak looked differently, and it was on ground that actually had been entered only by cardinals in pursuit of spiritual endeavors or by others who work out of the convictions of the most positive and orthodox Catholicism. And so the air of the rooms where normally nothing but the official message from the orthodox center of Rome was proclaimed resounded with the free pronouncements of the spiritual scientific world view.

This shows us that although the free contemporary spirits of these Northern lands feel more attracted to anthroposophy, they can nevertheless look with a certain satisfaction to the souls who long to escape from an old, iron-clad orthodox tradition. It is certainly a good indication of the spirit of the times that it was possible to speak as freely and frankly about anthroposophic truths on territory heretofore reserved for cardinals, and as freely as this would be possible in the North. For what has been said before holds true everywhere: anthroposophy is sincerity; and where souls are in need of it and a call is issued, anthroposophy will follow it. But at no time will anthroposophy deviate in the least from the overall precepts that inspire its pronouncements, just because the consideration for the territory on which these pronouncements are made may make this expedient.

Wherever anthroposophical truth is proclaimed and where the spiritual element that pulsates through us is cultivated, there our message must be delivered in the light of sincerity, even when it is still surrounded by the thoughts of those who hate anthroposophy. However, in the midst of those who hate anthroposophy there are souls who, more or less consciously, long for the light of anthroposophy. And especially a strong contrast such as the one I have experienced during the past fourteen days can show us what a strong magnet anthroposophical life is.

The observation of our immediate present teaches us that this anthroposophical force is now strong enough to justify our joyful and satisfying hope that the small seedling planted today will in the future grow into a mighty tree. As theosophists, we are today in the same position humanity was in during the ancient Atlantean time. And just as life has become different since that time, so it will change again in the future, up to a time following a catastrophe. The wide perspective will now be made to appear before our souls.

Let us call to memory a similar movement in the last third of the Atlantean epoch that started small just like ours. The Atlantean soul life, which in many ways was still clairvoyant, had reached a high point during that time, but it did not yet have the consciousness of self, the strong feeling of the "I." Instead, Atlanteans had a certain ability of clairvoyance and also certain magical powers, and this enabled them to look into the spiritual world. Those who had progressed to be leaders of this civilization were the ones best able to gaze into the spiritual world in the old ways and to bring forth the most knowledge from the astral realms. This clairvoyance disappeared little by little; in fact, mankind had to lose it completely in order to conquer for itself the consciousness of self in the physical world. But it is certain that clairvoyant knowledge in the last third of the Atlantean era had reached a special climax.

You will remember the technological achievement of the Atlanteans. They flew over the earth in small space vehicles—close to the earth because the atmosphere was saturated with thick fog formations. They propelled their small vehicles through this sea of air and water with energy derived from sprouting plants. The leading creators of this technology can be compared to today's industrial wizards who construct ingenious machines from lifeless forces. And those Atlanteans who could relate the most from the spiritual world can be compared to today's leading scholars and natural scientists.

However, within this Atlantean humanity a segment of people began to evolve who had only minor clairvoyant faculties, but possessed the ability to regard the external world with affection. The first rudimentary beginnings of arithmetic and counting could be observed in these people, but their participation in the great advances of the Atlantean industry—the construction of ever mightier vehicles for this sea of water and air—was very limited. And thus a small, insignificant group of people had developed in this last third of the Atlantean period who, in a certain sense, were despised for their comparative lack of clairvoyant power and their inability to participate in this great industry. However, this group of people prepared the way for seeing and knowing that is prevalent today, the way of seeing and knowing of which the external world today is so proud since it developed it in such a one-sided way.

Those leaders of the Atlantean civilization who had mastered everything that could be known from the vantage point of the Atlantean consciousness, including technology, conceived of a technical idea toward the end of the Atlantean era that has become fully productive in modern times. We can compare it to another measure of progress in our time that will carry over into the next catastrophe. During their golden age, the Atlanteans had vehicles that moved through air that was heavily mixed with water. Later, however, when their culture was already in a state of decline, it also became necessary to navigate the water, and this led the last cultural races of the Atlantean era first to embracing and then to realizing the idea of navigation and the conquest of the seas. This momentous idea in the Atlantean era not only of traversing the air but also of navigating the ocean water was quite a sensational idea that was put into reality by the last Atlantean races. After long experiments to navigate the waters, success came during the time when Atlantean culture was already in its decline.

Those responsible for this tremendous progress were not the ones who could be recruited for the task of transmitting the legacy of the actual spiritual life from the Atlantean era to our time. Rather, this task was reserved for the plain and simple people because they had been the first ones to be endowed with the ability to relate to the physical world. They were the ones whose clairvoyant faculties, though deteriorated the most among the several groups of people, were still adequate for those who were messengers from the spiritual world. These people, despised by the great scholars and inventors, were gathered by an eminent initiate whom we call The Great Initiate of the Sun Oracle. This small group was comprised of people who had least preserved their technical abilities and who were disdained by the leaders and by the great scholars and inventors. Yet it was precisely they whom the Great Initiate of the Sun Oracle led from the West to the East, through Europe and into Asia. And it is also this small group of people that made the foundation of the post-Atlantean cultures possible.

The best of what was subsequently developed by the

various cultures, the mighty tree of post-Atlantean knowledge and wisdom, emanated from the descendants of the despised simple people from the Atlantean era. Above all, something else emanated from the midst of the descendants of this group of modest people. Let us place the external events side by side with the internal events of our evolution. Let us look at the great sensation of the Atlantean era when the secondary racial group, whose descendants were the Phoenicians, invented navigation. What was accomplished by this invention?

We need only to remember the great events from the beginning of modern times, such as the great voyages of discovery by Columbus and other seafarers, which would have been impossible without navigation and the invention of ships, and we shall see how this sensational invention led to the gradual conquest of the physical plane on earth. Post-Atlantean peoples were confined to a small radius of activities, but through the invention of ships the circle defining the earth became rounded out so that we now have a completed configuration of the physical plane. And thus, the sensational invention of the Atlantean world reaches into our time and promotes further progress on the physical plane.

However, the greatest conquest in the Atlantean era emanated from the descendants of that group of plain people gathered around the Great Initiate of the Sun Oracle. And when those descendants, through their own development, had prepared the Indian, Persian, Egyptian, Graeco-Latin, and our cultures, the earth became capable of yielding the material into which the Christ could be born. Therefore, the greatest spiritual event and deed of the post-Atlantean era had its beginning in the people who belonged to the most despised human beings in the eyes of the leaders of the Atlantean civilization, and this event gave rise to the immense spiritual progress that supports and maintains all spiritual life in our time—weaves through it and makes it productive.

The events in Atlantis are paralleled by those of our time. Seeing that the germinal beginnings of man's ability to do arithmetic and to count were present in Atlantis, we can recognize how these capabilities are today furthered in a marvelous conquest of the physical plane and how they brought about all kinds of technical progress. We also see how the great inventors and discoverers today have reached the culmination, in a sense, in applying those forces that first began to germinate with the small group of despised people in the Atlantean time. And what was then clairvoyant knowledge is today knowledge of nature and of the physical world. There is also a similarity between the spiritual leaders of the Atlantean civilization and today's natural scientists and scholars. On the other hand, a class of plain people exists everywhere—irrespective of positions its members might hold in the world, whose hearts are filled with the mighty magnet that attracts us to spiritual life, just as people in Atlantis were attracted to a life in which the external faculties for the physical plane could be developed.

Despite these similarities, there is also a certain difference between the modern and the ancient situation. In the old days referred to, the last remnants of clairvoyance were still present in people so that they were able to behold the Great Initiate. In a certain way, things today are more difficult for human beings when a call from the spiritual world issues to an equally small group of people, something we designate as the call of the Masters of Wisdom and of the Harmony of Feelings. But since people today are placed on the physical plane, these Masters of Wisdom and of the Harmony of Feelings are at first unknown to this small nucleus of human beings that has crystallized itself out of the mass of people. As we can deduce from the facts of the present time, this small group feels in its hearts that there is such a thing as a new spiritual message that is meant to have an effect on the future just as the message in former ages has had an effect on the present. These human beings who today come from all walks of life and whom we can find everywhere are the true theosophists because they carry in their hearts a longing for a spiritual life that is meant to lay the foundation for future cultures. The true theosophists in our time are emerging—just as we now encounter a sensational discovery similar to the one in the Atlantean era.

In ancient times water was conquered through the highest technological progress; the same is true today in the case of air. This conquest will, of course, extend into a later epoch. But just as ships in our times have brought about mastery of the physical plane only, so the air ship that will lead human beings into the atmosphere and beyond will empower the pilots to find only matter—material things. Granted, new realms of the physical plane will be conquered, and this will be beneficial for the external world. However, the inner spiritual life is borne in the hearts of those who feel spiritually fulfilled by the promise of being able in the future to look into the spiritual world while being conscious of self.

Look into life and you will find out there our leaders of civilization, the pillars of external culture, active as inventors and discoverers, as scholars and natural scientists. They look with scorn and contempt on a small group such as the one assembled here today that constitutes itself as a new bearer of culture and that unites its members with others in spiritual scientific associations. The events of the ancient Atlantean era repeat themselves.

However, when the spiritual life touches your hearts with such force that you can compare yourselves with dignity to those who were gathered around the Great Initiate of the Sun Oracle, then you will be the bearers of spiritual life in later ages. In addition to offering humanity the external, material, and corporeal realities, such a life would also make possible a renewed immersion in the spiritual world. Although the Great Initiate gathered human beings around Himself in ancient times, today the Masters of Wisdom and of the Harmony of Feelings fulfill a similar function and issue their call to you. If you feel your mission from a sense of history, then your hearts will become strong enough to withstand all the ridicule and disdain that the so-called pillars of civilization heap on Spiritual Science from the outside. And if you understand your mission in this spirit, then your thoughts will be strong and any doubt that may reverberate into your souls from the outside will be unable to shake you in your conviction. Your thoughts will be spiritually refined by the very force that can issue from such a knowledge of our mission. Even if we have to review thousands of years and establish far-reaching ideals, it is worth the effort because where such ideals are established, life is transmuted, and where they are absent, life is dead. Ideals transform themselves into the force of a moment even if they have been taken from vast periods of time and may seem to make the person subscribing to them appear somewhat petty and despondent. You will be strong for the most insignificant task if you are capable of extracting your ideal from the loftiest heights. This will make you stand fast when those who govern the world with their erudition talk with disdain and contempt about the little spiritual scientific associations where those people sit who "do not want to go along with contemporary culture." Oh yes, they do want to go along, and they also know to appreciate the accomplishments of the external, physical world, but they also know that just as a body cannot be without a soul, no external culture can exist without spiritual life.

Just as the despised human beings characterized above gathered around the Great Initiate and after generations

79

made the existence of Christ on earth possible, so the anthroposophical movement must facilitate a comprehensive understanding of Christ. Christ descended to earth in the fourth major era, and those who wish to understand Him completely will be able to do so from the anthroposophical vantage point.

Why do people who have heretofore been nourished by the positive, orthodox religions, come to Spiritual Science as if responding to an undefined longing in their consciousness? Why do they listen to the anthroposphical message when before they listened only to the Vatican? Why? Is it still permissible today to say anthroposophy exists only for those who regard the greatest spiritual fact of our age—the Christ Impulse—with indifference? What do the people coming to us need from us? They want us to tell them who Christ was and what He accomplished! They are coming to us because those who consider themselves to be the privileged bearers of the Christ-name today cannot tell them who Christ was, whereas anthroposophy can. Today's cultural leaders use the denial of Christ to oppose the external tradition emanating from various religions, but they cannot effectively challenge the moribund positive religious movements. Those who do not know what the Great Christ is, those who deny His spirituality will be no match even for the old religious movements. But only the spiritual movements that place themselves in the midst of those who claim an exclusive right to the Christ-name, the movements who know how to express the true essence of the Christ even to those who wish to hear the opposite, only those spiritual movements will attract human beings to their cause who carry the future in their hearts. The ancient religious trends will prove to be stronger than all religious nihilism.

We do not conceive of anthroposophical life in a petty, dogmatic sense, nor do we want to comprehend it with the help of individual tenets or maxims, but rather by recognizing and understanding the mission and the task of our time. We want to embrace anthroposophical life in such a way that the true spirit of our time speaks to us and that the most significant event of our post-Atlantean era can be expressed through the words of anthroposophy. If these words are not just recited but rather put into practice as an expression of the spirit of our time, they will become a dynamic force of life in our souls, and this will make people understand what anthroposophical life is.

When we truly feel this, we will increasingly grow stronger, and the newly gained strength will help us to embrace our ideal firmly. Then we will know how this ideal can be justified, regardless of whether this happens in an environment where an old culture yearns for a new content, or in this environment here, where nature and the magnificent, spirit-endowed sunrays glittering around us encircle what the daily efforts of anthroposophy achieve. We will again learn to recognize the spirit within these sunrays and know that when the sun has set, the spirit indwelling in it will look into our hearts. We will also learn what it means to behold the sun and its spirit at midnight, and in understanding what this spirit is, we will see how it has descended and how it is now united with the highest impulses of our age. It is necessary that humanity understand the Christ-Impulse and that we can say who the Christ was. Such an understanding is now only in the beginning stages, but in direct proportion to its increasing spiritual insights, mankind will gradually understand how the Christ-Impulse has penetrated this worldly edifice.

To feel this way at the dedication of a branch of our movement is especially appropriate when, as is the case here, the members were united in wanting to express a heartfelt desire and name this branch after Francis of Assisi, whose life is enveloped by a deep spiritual mystery.

When Christ descended to the earth, He enveloped

81

Himself with the threefold physical, etheric, and astral bodies of Jesus of Nazareth and lived three years in this sheath as Christ, the Sun-Spirit. With the event of the Mystery of Golgotha, Christ descended to the earth; but aside from what is known to all of you, something else special happened by virtue of the fact that Christ indwelled the three bodies of Jesus of Nazareth, particularly the astral and etheric bodies. After Christ cast off the bodies of Jesus of Nazareth, they were still present as spiritual substance in the spiritual world, but multiplied in a great many copies. They did not perish in the world ether or in the astral world, but continued to live as identical images. Just as the seed of a plant, once buried in the ground, reappears in many copies according to the mystery of number, so the copies of Jesus of Nazareth's etheric and astral bodies were present in the spiritual world. And for what purpose were they present, considering the large framework of spiritual economy? They were there to be preserved and to serve the overall progress of the human race.

One of the first individuals to benefit from the blessed fact of these countless copies of Jesus's etheric body being present in the spiritual world was St. Augustine. When he again descended to earth after an earlier incarnation, not just any etheric body was woven into his own, but rather the copy of the etheric body of Jesus of Nazareth. Augustine had his own astral body and ego, but his etheric body was interwoven with the image of the etheric body of Jesus. He had to work through the culture of his ego and astral body, but when he had made his way to the etheric body, he realized the great truths that we find in his mystical writings.

Many other human beings from the sixth to the ninth centuries had a copy of the etheric body of Jesus woven into their own etheric bodies. Many of these individuals conceived the Christian images that later were to be glorified in the arts in the form of the Madonna or the Christ on the cross.

They were the creators of religious images who experienced in themselves what the people living at the time of the Mystery of Golgotha had experienced.

In the period spanning the eleventh through the fifteenth centuries the time had come when a copy of the astral body of Jesus of Nazareth was woven into the astral bodies of certain reincarnated souls. From the eleventh to the fourteenth centuries many human beings, for example Francis of Assisi and Elisabeth of Thüringen, had the imprint of the astral body of Jesus of Nazareth woven into them while their own astral bodies—the source of their knowledge—were formed during reincarnation. This enabled these individuals to proclaim the great truths of Christianity in the form of judgments, logical constructs, and scientific wisdom. But, in addition, they were also able to experience the feeling of carrying the astral body of Jesus of Nazareth within themselves.

Your eyes will be opened if you allow yourselves to experience vicariously all the humility, the devotion, and the Christian love that was part of Francis of Assisi. You will then know how to look at him as a person prone to make mistakes—because he possessed his own ego—and as a great individual because he carried a copy of the astral body of Jesus of Nazareth within his own astral body. All the humble feelings, the profound mysticism, and the spiritual soul life of Francis of Assisi become comprehensible if we know this one secret of his life.

Having such knowledge, we can see with our inner eye that the future of this new branch augurs well as it climbs upward under the guiding light of this great individual, for those who, like Francis of Assisi, received the grace and the calling to guide Christian humanity in the West will at all times let their spiritual light radiate into the areas of spiritual activity. And especially if this Francis of Assisi Section works in a genuinely spiritual sense, the unison of thoughts and feelings of this branch will be the reflection of the harmonizing light of Francis of Assisi, which he received as a gift of grace, as we mentioned before, by an infusion of his own astral body with a copy of the astral body of Jesus of Nazareth. Something of this light will radiate into this very branch.

In letting such perspectives roll by our inner eye, we who are assembled today in this modest branch for the purpose of dedicating the new branch will leave the proper feelings behind us when we depart. Let us look up to the light of Francis of Assisi; let us take along with us what can be ignited in us in this moment, and let us remember this branch in the future. In doing so, our feelings and thoughts will hover invisibly over this Francis of Assisi Branch, so that the impulses struggling upward from below may prove to be worthy of the light that shines into our souls from the outside. In such a moment we become conscious of the fact that we are here to work for the true and real measures of progress in our post-Atlantean era. Surely, when the founders of this branch felt the need to name it after Francis of Assisi, their souls must have sensed something of the great progress.

What was the most decisive turning point of our entire evolution? It was the time when the Christ descended to earth. Let us look back six hundred years from that event and then compare the earth to what it was six hundred years after Christ, a period spanning some twelve hundred years. First, let us look at Buddha, who lived six hundred years before Christ. In him we see an individuality of such greatness that words of admiration should be superfluous. Specifically, let us look at the moment where he is led out into life, but not into the life he wanted to live. Consider how he first meets a helpless child and how from this experience he forms the perception that there is suffering in the journey that human beings begin with their birth. And upon seeing a sick person, he says to himself, "Not only is there suffering in this world, but human beings on this plane are also subjected to illness.'' He sees an old person who no longer is able to move his limbs and says to himself, ''Aging involves suffering.'' And when he sees a corpse, the sight of it conjures up in him the perception that death is suffering. Another perception is that to be separated from a loved one creates suffering, as is the case when one is united with someone whom one doesn't love. Finally, not to obtain what one desires is suffering too.

This, then, is the teaching that spread as the teaching of Buddha, some six hundred years before Christ. Let us fix in our minds the moment where Buddha steps out into the world, sees a corpse, and stands face to face with death. It was six hundred years after the event of Golgotha when for the first time one particular image came into being: the image of the cross with the corpse of the Savior hanging on it. Thousands of people were there to look at it. Now when Buddha looked at a corpse, it was to him a personification of all suffering on earth. The believers of the Christian community six hundred years after Christ would look at the corpse and see it as the victory of all spiritual life over death, the claim to bliss. And here we see how a faithful community looked at a dead body six hundred years before Christ, and then six hundred years after the event of Golgotha.

What can the Christ-Event tell us about the other pronouncements of suffering? Is birth suffering, as Buddha expressed it? Looking at Christ on the cross, the part of humanity that really understands Him will say, ''Through birth we step into this existence—an existence that was found worthy of harboring the Christ. We are born into a life in which we can unite with Christ.'' Likewise, sickness is not suffering if one understands Christ. People will have to learn to understand through the Christ-Impulse what, from a spiritual point of view, creates health. Illnesses will be healed in a spiritual way through the innermost, Christianized life. By dying to the outer world, we become assured that the treasure acquired in connection with the Christ-Impulse is carried into every other life. Through Christ's victory, death appears to us as a bridge that leads to the spiritual world, and we learn to understand the meaning of death for this spiritual world through this Christ-Impulse.

Also, it is no longer possible to say that the separation from the object of one's love creates suffering because the power of Christ will unite us, as one soul to another, with everything we want to love. Moreoever, the power of Christ will tie those together who love each other. The suffering that could arise through the separation of those loving each other is overcome through Christ.

Let us learn to love all people, lest our interpretation of the world be that to be united with what one does not love means suffering. Rather, let us learn to love every creature in its own right, and when our spiritual wells start to flow, our desires will be purified in such a way that we can partake in everything our souls are destined to receive, once the hurdles of the physical world are eliminated. And those spiritual fountainheads can begin to flow through the Christ-Impulse. People who will be content to obtain through the Christ-Spirit what they want will have their desires purified.

The new spiritual life has placed itself next to the old spiritual life through the Christ-Impulse. That is how deep progress in spiritual life ran before and after the Christ-Impulse had surfaced. This is keenly felt by someone who turns to one of the most ardent and joyful admirers and messengers of the Christ-Impulse—Francis of Assisi; his name, therefore, may well be bestowed on an association in which spiritual life is to be cultivated. May this name be a good augury, and may the work in this branch proceed in the true spirit of our time, properly understood, because this is necessary for the programs we have envisioned in our souls.

Let us consecrate this branch of our movement in the

spirit expressed by the preceding words and by calling down the benediction we used yesterday when we broke ground for the outer temple. Let us conjure up the same spirit one more time so that it may hold sway and weave in this Francis of Assisi Branch.

May the feelings of those who have come to this dedication ceremony unite with this spirit and also unite in a brotherly way with those who are at work here in serious, anthroposophical endeavors so that spiritual life may germinate in the midst of the trees, forests, and sprouting plants of this sunny piece of nature. It matters little whether the bright sunrays outside indicate what is beautiful or magnificent in nature, whether snow be piled up outside, or whether a thick cloud cover be out there to obscure the external, physical sunlight. In times when nature renews itself or when she wears her somber garb, may the spirit of a higher life always imbue those who will be engaged in spiritual activities, and let us now conjure up this spirit to aid all the human beings in this branch.

With this, let us dedicate, from the bottom of our hearts, the Francis of Assisi Branch and hope that it will continue its work in the spirit in which it began—through the spiritual force of the Masters of Truth and of the Harmony of Feelings that streams into every branch. May it also continue its work through the good spirit with which it has endowed itself by naming itself after the splendid bearer of Christ.

May this branch continue as it began. Good spirits will guide its course as it becomes one of the centers where the kind of life is cultivated of which our time is clearly in need and where the seeds for the requirements of a far-distant future are sown. Let us hope the people who will soon have to work in solitude here emerge strengthened from today's festivities, where so many sincere friends united their feelings with them! Then the spiritual life cultivated in this place will flow back to all people involved and coalesce with

87

the great harmony of anthroposophical life. Thoughts that originate in this place will encounter our thoughts, just as our thoughts will flow here from distant places. This harmony is something like an external garment of spirituality, and spirituality must pass through human evolution like a spiritual breath of air if beneficial forces are to reign over humanity.

May this branch be dedicated in the fullest sense of the word; may it become a field of activity into which we can always place our hopes with the same love and inner satisfaction as is the case in today's dedication ceremony.

Lecture VII

The Macrocosmic and the Microcosmic Fire:
The Spiritualization of Breath and Blood

Cologne, April 10, 1909

Goethe,[35] one of the most inspired spirits in modern times, knew how to depict in a touching way the strength and the power of sounds at Easter—the sound of the Easter bells. When his character Faust, the representative of striving humanity, has reached the outer limit of earthly existence, he seeks death. Goethe, however, also makes clear to us how the sounds of Easter bells, similar to the brightness of Easter itself, can conquer the thought and the impulse of death in Faust's heart.

The inner impulse of the sounds of Easter that Goethe places before us is the same impulse that passed through the entire development of humanity. In the not too distant future, human beings will understand through a renewed absorption in spiritual things how our festivals are intended to connect the human soul with everything that weaves into and lives in the universe. Then people will feel in a new way how their souls expand with joy during these first days of spring and understand the manner in which the sources of spiritual life can liberate us from the material world and from the narrowness of an existence that is tied to material things.

Especially during Easter will the human soul feel most fervently how an unshakable faith is being poured into it, which indicates that there is a well of the eternal, divine existence deep inside every human being. This fountainhead removes us from all constrictions and allows us to be one with the source of universal existence without losing ourselves. We can find a new life in this source at any time, provided we are able to rise to its knowledge through illumination. That which constitutes the true essence of Easter is nothing but an external sign of the Christian Mystery, the most profound experience mankind has ever had. And thus, we feel at this time of the year as if the external festivities and the manifestations of Easter were a symbol of the truths that human beings were able to discover only at the beginning of evolution, as well as a symbol of the knowledge that was available to them exclusively from the depths of the Holy Mysteries. What we call Easter was widely celebrated by ancient peoples, and wherever it was celebrated, it grew out of the Holy Mysteries. And everywhere such celebrations conjured up the notion and the conviction that the life that is lived in the spirit can conquer death, because death resides in the material world. In whatever way the human soul became convinced of this truth in ancient times, the substance of this conviction was ultimately derived from the very core of the Holy Mysteries.

However, the progression of human evolution consists precisely in the fact that the secrets formerly known only to holy places and to the Mystery Centers are now increasingly accessible to all of humanity and will eventually become common knowledge. In today's and tomorrow's festivities we will therefore observe, and attempt to present, how this notion—this feeling—was at first confined to the few in ancient times but has increasingly gained ground in the course of human development and is now known to an ever increasing number of people. Today let us look back into the past so that tomorrow we will be able to describe the feelings people in our time have toward Easter.

Our Christian Easter is only one among humanity's

many forms of celebrating Easter, and what the sages of mankind had to say about conquering death through life was a result of the strongest convictions and sprang from the deepest wells of wisdom. These insights were built into the Easter symbols, and we find there elements that are designed to awaken in us an understanding of Easter, of the resurrection feast of the spirit. A beautiful and deep oriental legend tells us the following.

Shakyamuni, the Buddha, was a great oriental teacher who made many oriental regions happy with his deep wisdom. Since this wisdom had sprung from the primeval wells of spiritual existence, it warmed the hearts of humanity and filled them with utter bliss. Shakyamuni preserved for later ages that ancient wisdom of the divine-spiritual worlds that had beatified the hearts of human beings when they were still able to look into the divine world. The Buddha had one great disciple, Kashyapa, who was able to understand his teachings, whereas his other disciples were more or less incapable of grasping the comprehensive wisdom taught by Buddha. He was one of the initiates most profoundly in tune with the teaching of Buddha and one of his most important successors. The legend tells us that when it was time for Kashyapa to die and when, because of his maturity, he was ready to enter the state of Nirvana, he went out to a steep mountain and hid in a cave. There his body remained after his death in an imputrescible state; only the initiates knew about this secret and about the location of Kashyapa's body. However, Buddha himself had once predicted the coming of Maitreya-Buddha, his great successor who was to become the new teacher and leader of humanity and who, when he had reached the zenith of his preordained earthly existence, would seek out the cave of the illumined Kashyapa to touch his imperishable corpse with the right hand. Then from the heavens a fire would stream down in which Kashyapa's body would be transported to the spiritual world.

The very degree by which the oriental legend differs

91

from what we know as the content of the Easter story affords us an opportunity to gain a deeper understanding of Easter. Only through a gradual approach can we grasp the primeval wisdom contained in this legend. We could begin by asking why Kashyapa—in contradisctinction to the Savior in the Christian report of Easter—does not conquer death after three days; or we might ask why the corpse of the oriental initiate remains in this imperishable state for such a long period of time until it is finally moved upward to the celestial spheres by a miraculous fire.

Today we can only allude to the hidden depths of such things, and only little by little can we get an idea of the wisdom expressed in such profound legends. It is especially important at festivals such as Easter to keep a modest and respectful distance and to gradually raise our consciousness to the heights of wisdom by engaging ourselves in the ritual of celebration. We must not give in to the temptation of wanting to grasp the meaning of these legends quickly with our dry intellect. No, these truths can be approached and ultimately understood only by gradually attuning our perceptive sensibilities and feelings to them. Only after this ripening process can we grasp the great truths with the zeal and full warmth of our sensibilities.

For today's humanity, two closely related truths shine as mighty lights and emblems on the horizon of the spirit—important points of reference for a developing humanity that is striving within the spiritual realm. The first emblem is the burning bramblebush of Moses, and the second is the fire appearing under lightning and thunder at Sinai from which Moses received the pronouncement of the *"I am the I am."*[36] Who is that spiritual being in the two apparitions announcing himself to Moses?

Anyone who understands the Christian message in a spiritual sense will also understand the words that announce to Moses the Being in the burning bramblebush, and later in the fire on Mt. Sinai—the Being who places the Ten Commandments before his soul. The writer of the Gospel of St. John tells us that Moses prophesied the Coming of Christ Jesus, and the Evangelist John expressly lets him point to those places in the Bible where the force in the burning bramblebush and later in the fire at Sinai announces Himself as the Being who was later to be named "the Christ." No godhead other than the Christ is intended to be introduced by the words *"I am the I am."*

The God who later appeared in the human body and who confronted mankind with the Mystery of Golgotha reigns invisibly after He had announced Himself earlier in the fire element in nature, in the burning bush, and in the lightning fire of Sinai. And you can understand the Old or the New Testament only if you know that the God proclaimed by Moses is the Christ who was supposed to walk among people. That is how the God who is supposed to bring salvation to human beings announces Himself in a way as no being in human form would. He announces Himself in the fiery element of nature, the element in which Christ is living. His divine essence makes itself known in many forms. The same Divine Being that reigns throughout all of antiquity now makes His visible appearance through the Event in Palestine.

Let us look back to the Old Testament and ask ourselves whom the ancient Hebrews actually revered. Who is their God? The members of the Hebrew Mystery Centers knew it; they worshiped the Christ and recognized Him as the speaker of the words, "Tell my people: *I am the I am.*" But even if nothing of this were known, the very fact that God, within our cycle of humanity, announced Himself in the fire would be sufficiently authentic evidence to the person capable of seeing into the deep mysteries of nature that the God of the burning bramblebush is identical with the God who announced Himself on Mt. Sinai. He came down from spiritual heights in order to fulfill the Mystery of Golgotha through His descent into a human body. For there is a mysterious connection between the fire that ignites the elements of nature out there and the fire that pulsates through our blood in the form of body temperature. We have often emphasized in our Spiritual Science that the human being is a microcosm juxtaposed to the large world, the macrocosm. Therefore, when we perceive things in the right way, the inner processes of a human being must correspond to processes taking place outside in the universe. For every inner-process we must be able to find the corresponding outer process, but to understand the meaning of this requires that we enter deep shafts of Spiritual Science. We are touching here the fringe of a deep mystery, of a truth that answers this question: What in the external macrocosm corresponds to the origin of human thought within us?

Human beings are the only creatures on earth who really think, and through their thoughts they are able to experience a world that extends beyond the earth. The manner in which thoughts flash up in the human being has no parallel in any other creature on earth. What is taking place within us when a thought is ignited, when either the simplest or the most enlightening thought flashes into our minds? To answer this question, let us say that the ego and astral body are simultaneously activated within us when we let our thoughts pass through our souls. Our blood is the physical expression of our ego, and that which in our nervous system is called "life" is the physical expression of our astral body. Not a single thought would flare up in our souls if ego and astral body did not work in concert, thus giving rise to a commensurate, interdependent functioning of the blood and of the nervous system. The future science of human beings will some day be amazed at today's scientific theory, which holds that thoughts originate solely in the nervous system. This belief is incorrect because the process responsible for the origination of thoughts must be seen as a dynamic interaction between blood and nervous system.

A thought flashes up in our soul when our blood, our inner fire, nervous system, and air cooperate in such a way. The origination of the thought inside our soul corresponds to rolling thunder in the cosmos. Likewise, when lightning flashes in the air, and when air and fire interact to produce thunder, this corresponds to the fire of our blood and the activity of our nervous system. This produces what one might metaphorically call an inner thunder that echoes in our thoughts, albeit gently, quietly, and imperceptibly. The lightning in the clouds corresponds to the fire and to the warmth in our blood, whereas the air outside, including all the elements it contains in the universe, corresponds to everything that passes through our nervous system. And just as lightning in its counterplay with the elements produces thunder, so the counterplay of blood and nerves produces the thought that flashes up in the soul. Suppose we looked out into the world that surrounds us, saw lightning flashing up in the air, and heard rolling thunder discharging itself. Then suppose that, as we looked into our soul, we sensed an inner warmth pulsating in our blood and felt the life that passes through our nervous system, a thought would flash up within us to tell us that both the external and the internal event were one.

That is really the truth! Although our thoughts take place within ourselves, the thunder rolling in the sky is not just a physical, material phenomenon. To assert that it was so would be nothing but materialistic mythology. However, individuals able to perceive that spiritual beings weave and radiate through material existence will look up to the sky, see the lightning, hear the thunder, and to them this will be a true and real indication of God's thinking in the fire, of His intention to announce Himself to us. That is the invisible God who weaves and radiates through the universe. His warmth is in the lightning, His nerves in the air, His thoughts in the rolling thunder; and it was He who spoke to Moses in the burning bramblebush and in the lightning fire of Sinai.

The elements fire and air in the macrocosm correspond to blood and nerves in the human microcosm. Thoughts in the human being are what lightning and thunder are in the macrocosm. By analogy, the God whom Moses saw and heard in the burning bush and who spoke to him in the lightning fire of Mt. Sinai appears as the Christ in the blood of Jesus of Nazareth. By thinking like a human being and by being in a human body, Christ's influence as the great model for human evolution extends into the far-distant future. And thus, two poles in the human evolution meet each other: the macrocosmic God on Mt. Sinai who announces Himself in thunder and lightning fire, and the same microcosmic God who is embodied in the human being of Palestine.

The sublime mysteries of humanity have been derived from the most profound wisdom. They are not invented legends, but a truth so profound that we need all the means available to Spiritual Science in order to unveil the mysteries that are woven around this truth. Let us ask what kind of an impulse mankind received through its great model, the Christ-Being, who descended to earth and united Himself with the microcosmic copies of the elements that are present in the human body.

Let us look back one more time to the prophecies of ancient cultures. All of them, back to the very distant past of the post-Atlantean era, probably knew what the course of human development would be. The Mystery Centers everywhere taught what is now proclaimed by Spiritual Science as follows: Human beings consist of four parts: the physical, the etheric, and the astral bodies, and the ego. They can rise to higher stages of development: through individual effort on the part of their ego, when they transform their astral body into spirit self—*manas*, when they transform their etheric body into life spirit—*buddhi*, and when they spiritualize the physical body into spirit man—*atman*. All the members of this physical body must be gradually spiritualized in our life on earth so that everything that makes human beings out of us through the influx of the divine breath is profoundly spiritualized. And because spiritualization of the physical body begins with the spiritualization of the breath—of the *odem*, the transformed, spiritualized physical body is called *atma* or *atman*, from which the German word for breath, *atem*, derives. The Old Testament tells us that the human being received the breath of life in the beginning of his earthly existence. Likewise, all ancient Schools of Wisdom perceived this breath of life as something that must gradually be spiritualized by the human being, and they saw *atman* as a deification of the breath—as the great ideal human beings must strive for—so that they will be imbued with the spiritual breath of air.

But there is still more in the human being that has to be spiritualized. If the entire body is to be spiritualized, it is necessary not only that the breath be spiritualized but also that the blood—the expression of the ego that is constantly renewed by the breath—be spiritualized. The blood must be infected by a strong impulse toward the spiritual. Christianity has added to the ancient mysteries the mystery of the blood and of the fire that is enclosed in the human being. The ancient mysteries say that human beings have descended to earth in their present earthly form and physical corporeality from spiritual heights. Having lost their spiritual essence and having wrapped themselves into a physical corporeality, they must return to spirituality by casting off the physical sheath and by ascending to a spiritual existence.

The religions could not teach what one might call the self-induced salvation of the human ego as long as the ego,

97

whose physical expression is in the blood, was not touched by an impulse now present on earth. And thus we are told how the great spiritual beings—the great avatars—descend and incarnate themselves from time to time in human bodies, especially when humanity needs help. These are beings who do not need to descend into a human body to enhance their own development because they have completed their own human development in an earlier cycle of the world. They descend for the sole purpose of helping human beings. For example, when mankind is in need of help, the great god Vishnu descends from time to time into an earthly existence. Krishna, one of the incarnations of Vishnu, speaks of himself and explains clearly what the essence of an avatar is. In the divine poem, the *Bhagavad Gita*, he himself explains what he is. Here we have the wonderful words that Krishna, in whom Vishnu lives as an avatar, says about himself: "I am the spirit of creation, its beginning, its middle, its end; I am the Sun among the stars, fire among the elements, the great ocean among the waters, the eternal snake among all snakes. I am the basis of everything."[37]

No words can proclaim more beautifully and more magnificently the all-embracing, omnipotent divinity. The godhead whom Moses saw in the elements of fire not only weaves and radiates through the macrocosmic world but also can be found inside the human being. That is why the Krishna-Being indwells in anything human as the great ideal to which the human core strives to develop itself from within. And if, as the wisdom of antiquity endeavored to do, the human breath can be spiritualized through the impulse that we absorb through the Mystery of Golgotha, then we have realized the principle of salvation through that which itself lives within us. All avatars saved mankind through the forces they caused to radiate from spiritual heights down onto earth. The avatar Christ, however, saved mankind by means of

98

what He Himself extracted from the strength of mankind, and He showed us how the strength to be saved and to conquer matter through spirit can be found within ourselves.

Now we can see how even such an illuminate as Kashyapa could not yet be fully saved even though he had made his body imperishable. This body of his had to remain in the secret cave until the Maitreya-Buddha came to pick it up. Only when the physical body has been so spiritualized through the ego that the Christ-Impulse can stream into it does one no longer need the wonderful cosmic fire in order to attain salvation; what is needed for salvation is the fire raging in the blood of the inner human being. And that is why we can utilize the light that radiates from the Mystery of Golgotha in order to illuminate such a wonderfully profound legend as the one told about Kashyapa.

At first blush, the world appears to us dark and full of riddles, but we can compare it with a dark room containing many splendid objects that we are unable to see when we first enter. However, when we ignite a light, it illuminates the whole splendor of the objects in the room and everything else represented by these objects. The same can be true for the human being who strives for wisdom. The human being strives at first in the dark; looking in this world first to the past and then to the future, he or she can at first see nothing but darkness. However, once the light coming from Golgotha is ignited, everything from the farthest past to the remotest future becomes illuminated. Since everything material is born out of the spirit, the spirit will again rise from matter. To express this certainty is the meaning of today's celebration of Easter—a festival that is tied to the events of the world. Mankind must realize what it can attain through Spiritual Science: if the human soul, by gaining knowledge of the mysteries of existence, can acquire a lively feeling for the mysteries of the universe on important symbolic occasions such as Easter, then it will also feel something of what it means to live not simply in one's own narrow, personal existence but also in a symbiosis with the light of the stars, the splendor of the sun, and with everything that lives in the universe. The soul will become increasingly more spiritual as it feels extended into the universe.

The spiritual Easter bells echo their sounds through our hearts, indicating that we must pass from a human to a universal life through the resurrection. Hearing these spiritual Easter bells will make us lose any doubt we may have about the spiritual world, and we will then be sure that death in the material world cannot harm us. When we understand these spiritual Easter bells, we will return to the life in the spirit.

Lecture VIII

The Event of Golgotha
The Brotherhood of the Holy Grail
The Spiritualized Fire

Cologne, Easter Sunday, April 11, 1909

One immediate advantage of significant time symbols
such as Easter is that this festival makes our hearts and souls
more amenable to the process of looking more and more
deeply into the human riddles and into human nature.
Therefore, let us once more place before our spiritual eye
the oriental legend that illumined our souls yesterday since
it has already given us a notion that it can disclose something
of the human riddles and the nature of the human being.
This is the legend of the great sage Kashyapa, the inspired
disciple of Shakyamuni. Kashyapa had encompassed all the
wisdom of the Orient with great purview and with an enormous impulse of activity. Of him it was rightly said that
none of his successors were even faintly capable of preserving what he had recovered from Shakyamuni's deep well of
wisdom or of preserving what he, Kashyapa—the last one to
do so—had given mankind from the primordial wisdom of
the world.

Let us continue the legend. When death approached,
Kashyapa felt that he was close to Nirvana and went to a
cave of the mountain. After he had died there in full consciousness, his physical body remained in an imperishable
state but could be discovered only by those who had become

101

mature enough to penetrate such secrets. While Kashyapa's imperishable body lay mysteriously concealed in that mountain cave, it was prophesied that a new great proclaimer of the primordial world wisdom would appear in the form of the Maitreya-Buddha who, upon reaching the summit of his earthly existence, was to go to the cave that contained Kashyapa's corpse. He would touch Kashyapa with his right hand, and then a wondrous fire was to come down from the universe, envelop the imperishable body of Kashyapa, and carry him into the higher spiritual worlds.

The oriental who understands such wisdom expects the reappearance of Maitreya-Buddha and his action on the imperishable body of Kashyapa. Will these two events really occur? Will the Maitreya-Buddha appear? And if he does, will the imperishable remains be moved upward through the wondrous heavenly fire? We will be able to get a presentiment of the deep wisdom that is embedded in this legend if we dwell in our true Easter feelings and visit the wondrous fire that is to absorb Kashyapa's remains.

Yesterday we saw how the godhead reveals Himself in our time through two poles: on the one hand through the macrocosmic lightning fire, and on the other hand through the microcosmic fire of the blood. We have seen that the Christ announced Himself to Moses in the burning bramble-bush and in the thunder and lightning fire on Sinai. No other force but Christ spoke to Moses, announced Himself as the *I am the I am*, and from the lightning fire at Sinai gave the Ten Commandments to him. After He had manifested Himself in this way, He appeared in the microcosmic pole in Palestine. The fire that lives in our blood contains the same God who announced Himself in the celestial fire and who then incarnated in a human body in the Mystery of Palestine so that he could imbue with His force the blood that contains the human fire. And if we follow the consequences this event has for earthly existence, we will be able

102

to find through this event the blazing fire that will accept the remains of Kashyapa.

All developments in the course of the world are such that material things become spiritualized little by little. An external sign of God's power appeared to Moses in the material fire of the burning bramblebush and on Mt. Sinai. However, this fire was spiritualized through the Christ-Event, and who is able to perceive the burning spiritual fire after the Christ-Force infused itself into the earth? Only the spiritual eye that has been opened and awakened through the Christ-Impulse can see this fire because it sees this sensuous fire of the bramblebush in an etherealized and spiritualized form. And after the Christ-Impulse awakened the spiritual eye of human beings, this fire has also had a spiritual effect on our world.

When was this fire again perceived? It was perceived again when Saul opened his eyes on his way to Damascus, found that they had become illumined and clairvoyant, and recognized in the heavenly fire the One who had accomplished the Mystery of Golgotha. Both Saul, who became Paul, and Moses saw the Christ. Moses saw Him in the material fire—in the burning thornbush and in the lightning fire on Sinai—and only his inner being could tell him that the Christ spoke to him. On the other hand, Christ appeared to the enlightened eye of Paul from the spiritual and etherealized fire. Just as matter and spirit stand in a relationship to one another in the evolution of the world, there exists also in the course of the world a relationship between the mysterious fire of the bramblebush and of Sinai on the one hand, and the wondrous apparition of Saul on the other —that is, the fire that shines brightly to him from the clouds and transforms him into Paul. And what has this event done for the evolution of the world as a whole?

Let us look back to the large numbers of great personalities who were destined to beatify and save humanity. They

103

were the external expression of the avatars, the divine spiritual forces who descended from spiritual heights in various epochs and assumed a human form, such as Krishna, Vishnu, and others. These benefactors and saviors of mankind had to make their appearances so that humanity could find its way back into the spiritual worlds, and in ancient times it took the intercession of divine power to do so. However, when the Mystery of Golgotha happened, human beings received the ability to muster from within the strength necessary to elevate themselves and lead themselves upward into the spiritual worlds. The Christ descended much deeper than had those previous leaders of the world and of mankind: not only did He bring heavenly forces into the earthly body, but also He spiritualized this earthly body in such a way that it now became possible for human beings to find the way back into the spiritual world with the help of these very forces. Although the pre-Christian saviors had used divine powers, the Christ used human powers to save mankind. And with this act human forces have been placed before our souls in their primordial potential. What would have happened on our earth if the Christ had not appeared? This serious and deeply incisive question is the one we want to pursue today.

It doesn't matter how many world saviors might have descended from the spiritual worlds; in the final analysis, they all would have found down here only human beings who were so deeply struck in the material world and so entrenched in matter that the pure, divine-spiritual forces would have been unable to lift them upward out of this unholy, impure matter. The oriental sages were deeply distressed and looked sadly into the future, which they viewed this way: the Maitreya-Buddha will appear in order to renew the primeval wisdom of the world, but there will not be a disciple present to absorb such wisdom. If the course of the world had continued in such a fashion, the Maitreya-

Buddha would have preached to deaf ears and would not have been understood by human beings who were completely immersed in material things. The earth might well have become sufficiently materialistic to wither Kashyapa's body so that the Maitreya-Buddha would not have been capable of carrying Kashyapa's remains upward to divine-spiritual heights. The most knowledgeable individuals of oriental wisdom, then, were deeply saddened especially when they looked into the future and wondered whether the earth would still be capable of generating some understanding and feeling for the appearance of Maitreya-Buddha.

A strong heavenly force had to radiate into physical matter and sacrifice itself into this matter. What was required was more than just a God wearing the mask of human appearance; what was needed was a true human being with human powers who was carrying the God within himself. The Event of Golgotha had to happen so that the matter into which the human being was placed could be readied, cleansed, and ennobled. When components of matter are cleansed and sanctified, this will make the comprehension of primordial wisdom possible again in future incarnations. Mankind must be led to a true understanding of how the Event of Golgotha has really worked in this sense. How important has this event been to mankind, and how incisively has it affected the essence and the being of mankind?

Let us take a look at a period of twelve centuries: the six centuries before and the six centuries after the Event of Golgotha. And let us consider certain happenings that took place in human souls during that period of time. Truly, nothing more momentous and significant can be placed before the sensitive human soul than those powerful moments in the illumination of the Buddha, as they are related in the Buddha legend. He was not born in a stable, among poor shepherds, but left a royal environment in which he grew up. That fact alone is not what should be stressed, but rather the fact that he found he was unable to experience life in its various manifestations in such a royal environment.

He found a weak and wretched child whose birth into this existence had created nothing but suffering for the child, and so Buddha felt that birth is suffering. Then Buddha saw with his sensitive soul a sick person and so realized that this is what happens to a human being when he is carried into the earthly world because of his or her thirst for existence. He concluded that sickness was suffering. When he found an old man whose advanced age had made him an invalid, he asked himself: "What is this gift of life man has received that gradually makes him lose control over his limbs?" Old age was suffering. Upon seeing a corpse, Buddha confronted the powers of death to destroy and extinguish life, and he concluded that death, too, was suffering. As Buddha continued to look into the manifestations of life, he found that the separation from what one loved created suffering; to be united with what one did not love also created suffering; and, finally, suffering was caused by not receiving what one desired.

Buddha's doctrine of suffering had a mighty and vivid effect on the hearts of human beings. Countless people learned the great truth of being liberated from suffering through the extinction of the thirst for being, and they also learned how to strive outward from their earthly incarnations. Truly, the highest peak of human evolution is placed before our souls by such an endeavor.

Let us now view the period that comprises twelve centuries—six hundred years each before and after the birth of Christ. We need to stress that the Mystery of Golgotha took place in the middle of that period. From the age of Buddha, six hundred years before Golgotha, let us now call special attention only to what the Buddha felt at the sight of a corpse and what he taught in relation to this. Now that we have done this, let us immediately consider the time six hundred years after the Mystery of Golgotha, when countless souls and eyes turned to the cross on which a corpse was hanging. It is from this corpse that the impulses emanated that spiritualized life and signaled the glad tidings that death can be conquered by life. That, then, is the exact opposite of what Buddha felt when he saw a dead body.

Buddha saw in a corpse an indication of the insignificance and the futility of life. By contrast, the human beings six hundred years after the Event of Golgotha looked up to the corpse on the cross in a spirit of devout fervor. It was to them a sign of life, and their souls came to be imbued with the certainty that existence is not suffering, but that it carries over beyond death into a state of bliss. The crucified cross of the Christ Jesus six hundred years after the Event of Golgotha came to be a memorial symbol of life, of the resurrection of life, and of the victory over death and all suffering; six hundred years before the Mystery of Golgotha a corpse was the memorial symbol for the fact that human beings are subjected to misery and suffering because their thirst for being causes them to enter the physical world. Never has there been a more momentous reversal in the entire evolution of the human race.

If the human being's entry into the physical world had been considered as suffering six hundred years before the Event of Golgotha, how does the soul perceive the great truth of the misery of life after this event? How is this former truth perceived by people who look up to the cross of Golgotha with a high degree of understanding? Is birth suffering, as Buddha had said? Those who look up to the cross of Golgotha with a knowledgeable soul and who feel united with it will say to themselves: "This birth leads a human being into a world that had the opportunity to invest the Christ with its own elements." They were glad to enter this earth on which Christ had walked. And through the connection with Christ, the soul had gained the strength to

107

find its way up to the spiritual worlds, as well as the knowledge that birth is not suffering; birth is rather the gate through which one must pass to find the Savior—the Savior who has wrapped Himself into the same earthly materials that constitute the human physical sheath.

Is sickness suffering? Those who understood the Impulse of Golgotha in the true sense said: "No, it is not!" Even though mankind today cannot yet understand what the true spiritual life is that streams into them with Christ, people in the future will learn to understand it. They will know that a person whose innermost being is pervaded by the power of Christ, that an individual who allows himself or herself to become imbued with the Christ-Impulse will be able to overcome all illness with the help of the strong and healthy powers that he or she develops from within. This is so because Christ is the great healer of mankind. His power comprises everything that emanates from a spiritual well and is really able to develop the strong, healing power that can conquer illness. No, illness is not suffering, but rather an opportunity to overcome an impediment or a handicap by the development of the Christ-Force within us.

In the same way we must gain a clear understanding about the difficulties of old age. The weaker our limbs become, the greater the opportunity for us to grow in spirit and to master our infirmity through the power of Christ within us. Old age is not suffering because with every day we grow further into the spiritual world. And neither is death suffering because it is conquered in the resurrection. Death has been conquered through the Event of Golgotha.

Moreover, can we say that being separated from what we love constitutes suffering? No! The souls that imbue themselves with the Christ-Force know that love can forge indestructible spiritual bonds beyond all material hindrances. And there is nothing in life between birth and death and between death and rebirth to which we cannot spiritually find the way through the Christ-Impulse. If we imbue ourselves with the Christ-Impulse, it is unthinkable that we could possibly be separated from what we love in the long run. The Christ brings us together with what we love.

By the same token, "to be united with what we do not love" cannot be suffering because the Christ-Impulse teaches us that once we have accepted it into our souls, we must love everything in its own measure. The Christ-Impulse shows us the way, and when we have found this way, "to be united with what we do not love" can never cause suffering for then there will no longer be anything that we do not embrace lovingly. And "not to attain what one desires" can no longer be suffering either if one embraces Christ, for the human sensibilities, feelings, and desires are purified and ennobled by the Christ-Impulse in such a way that human beings desire only what they are meant to receive. They no longer suffer from the lack of things, for if they are meant to do without something or someone, such lack is for their ennoblement; and the Christ-Power gives them the strength to perceive it as a purification. When this happens, the feeling of lacking things no longer evokes suffering.

So what is the Event of Golgotha? It is the gradual abolition of the teaching by the great Buddha that life is suffering. No other event has had a greater impact on the evolution and the nature of life in this world than the Event of Golgotha, and that is why we can understand that it will continue to work for mankind and have tremendous positive consequences for humanity in the future. Christ was the greatest avatar that ever descended to earth; and when such a being comes down into our existence, just as Christ descended into the body of Jesus of Nazareth, something mysterious and greatly significant happens. Let us look at the microcosmic world. When we put a grain of wheat into the ground, it germinates, grows a stalk, and many ears of wheat, and the many, many grains of wheat harvested are copies of the one grain originally planted in the ground. This process also takes place in the macrocosmic, spiritual world. For "all that is destructible is but a parable,"[38] and we can see in the multiplication of the wheat grain an image of, and a parable for, the spiritual worlds. And with this, we conclude our comparison. When the Event of Golgotha took place, something happened to the etheric body and the astral body of Jesus of Nazareth: they were multiplied through the power of the Christ that lived within Him, and many copies of the two bodies were henceforth present in the spiritual world and continued to be at work.

When a human individuality descends from spiritual heights into a physical existence, it envelops itself with an etheric body and with an astral body. But when something like the copies of the etheric and astral bodies of Jesus of Nazareth is present in the spiritual worlds, then something very special happens to human beings whose karma provides for this. After the Mystery of Golgotha had been accomplished, an individual whose karma permitted this received a copy of the etheric or the astral body of Jesus of Nazareth woven into himself or herself. This was the case in the first centuries of the Christian era, for example with St. Augustine. When such an individuality descended from spiritual heights and enveloped itself in an etheric body, it received a copy of the etheric body of Jesus of Nazareth woven into its own etheric body, but it had its own astral body and ego.

And thus, what had enveloped the God incarnate of Palestine now was carried over onto other human beings who were supposed to transfer the impetus of this great impulse to the rest of humanity. Since Augustine had to depend on his own ego and on his own astral body, he was subjected to doubts, ups and downs, and erroneous behavior; and since these shortcomings originated in the as-yet-imperfect parts of his being, it was difficult for him to overcome them. What he had to go through was caused by errors in his judgment and by an erring ego. But after he had struggled through these problems and his etheric body began to be activated, he encountered forces within himself that had been woven into this etheric body from a copy of the etheric body of Jesus of Nazareth. And now he became the individual who was able to proclaim to the people in the West a part of the lofty mystery truths.

Thus many of the individuals whom we in the West know as the important pillars of Christianity were called upon to promote the active continuance of Christianity in the fourth, fifth, and sixth centuries, and on to the tenth century. These exemplary people were able to absorb the great ideas because their etheric bodies were interwoven with the etheric body of Jesus of Nazareth. It is for this reason that they were able to fathom the sublime visions and exemplary ideas that would later be put into artistic form by renowned painters and sculptors.

How did these exemplary types originate for the paintings that give us joy even today? They came into being when the human beings of the fifth, sixth, seventh, and eighth centuries after Christ received the great illuminations about Christianity that they did not have to comprehend with the help of historical accounts. Because of the copy of the sanctified etheric body of Jesus of Nazareth interwoven within them, these human beings were able to absorb the content of Christ's teaching without knowing the historically transmitted facts of Christianity. Because they bore a part of Jesus of Nazareth within themselves, they knew from a feeling of inner illumination that the Christ was alive. They knew it as well as Paul did when he saw the Christ-Apparition in the blazing spiritualized fire of the heavens. Was Paul before that occasion willing to be converted by force of the stories that circulated about the events in Palestine? None of the events anyone could have told him would have had the power of making a Paul out of Saul, and yet the most important impulse for the dissemination of Christianity emanated from Paul. He remained skeptical of the

111

stories about Christ on the physical plane and became a believer only through an occult event that took place in the spiritual world. Strange indeed are those people who want to have Christianity without spiritual illumination! The external expansion of Christianity was due to a supersensory event; it would never have taken place without Paul's spiritual illumination.

In later times, Christianity continued to grow through the activities of those who were able to experience the Christ, as described above, as a result of inner illumination, and these individuals were also capable of experiencing the historical Christ because they bore within themselves what had remained of the historical Christ and his bodies. During the time from the eleventh through the fourteenth centuries other individuals received copies of the astral, rather than the etheric, body of Jesus of Nazareth woven into themselves when they were mature enough and when their karma called for this. Francis of Assisi and Elisabeth of Thüringen, among others, were such human beings whose lives would remain incomprehensible to us unless we knew about this fact. Everything in the life of Francis of Assisi that appears to us strange stems from the fact that his ego was the human ego of this human individuality, but the humility, the devotion, and the fervor that we so admire in Francis of Assisi came from his having woven into his astral body a copy of the astral body of Jesus of Nazareth. Many other personalities of this time had such a copy woven into their own being; and when we know this, they become models for us to emulate. If a person were to get to the bottom of this matter without knowing that Elisabeth of Thuringen had a copy of the astral body of Jesus of Nazareth woven into herself, how could he or she fully understand the life of this saintly woman? Many, many individuals were called upon through this continuing Christ-Force to carry its mighty impulse into future ages.

In addition to copies of the etheric and of the astral body

of Jesus of Nazareth, countless copies of His ego were preserved for posterity as well. His ego had disappeared from the three sheaths when Christ moved into them, but a copy of this ego—heightened through the Christ-Event—remained and was multiplied into an infinite number of copies. We have in this copy of the ego of Jesus of Nazareth something that is still present today in the spiritual world, and human beings who have made themselves mature enough can find it and, with it, the splendor of the Christ-Force and of the Christ-Impulse that it carries within it.

The external expression for the ego is the blood. That is a great secret, but there have always been human beings who were acquainted with it and who were aware of the fact that copies of the ego of Jesus of Nazareth are present in the spiritual world. And since the Event of Golgotha, there have always been human beings through the centuries who had to see to it that humanity matured slowly to the point where some individuals could accept copies of the ego of Jesus Christ, just as some human beings received copies of His etheric or astral body. A secret way had to be found to preserve this ego in a silent, deep Mystery until the time when a suitable moment for its use would be at hand. To preserve this secret, a brotherhood of initiates was formed: The Brotherhood of the Holy Grail. This brotherhood goes back to the time when, as is reported, its founder took the chalice that Christ Jesus had used at the Last Supper and collected in it the blood that dripped from the wounds of the Savior when He was hanging on the cross. This founder of the brotherhood collected the blood of Christ Jesus, the expression and copy of His ego, in the chalice that is called the Holy Grail. It was kept in a holy place—in the brotherhood —that through its institution and initiation rites comprised the Brothers of the Holy Grail.

Today the time has come when these secrets can be revealed because the hearts of human beings can become ripened through spiritual life to an extent where they elevate

113

themselves to an understanding of this great mystery. If Spiritual Science can kindle souls so that they warm up to an engaged and lively understanding of such mysteries, these very souls will become mature enough, through casting a glance at that Holy Grail, to get to know the mystery of the Christ-Ego—the eternal ego into which any human ego can be transformed. This mystery *is* a reality. All that people have to do is to follow the call by Spiritual Science to understand this mystery as a given fact so that they can receive the Christ-Ego at the mere sight of the Holy Grail. To accomplish this, it is necessary only that one understand and accept these happenings as fact.

At a future time when people will be increasingly well-prepared to receive the Christ-Ego, it will imbue the souls of human beings to an ever increasing degree so that they can strive upward to approach the position where their great model Christ Jesus used to be. Only through this process will human beings learn to understand in what respect Christ Jesus is the great model of humanity, and only then will they begin to understand that the certainty and the truth of the life everlasting emanates from the corpse on the wooden cross at Golgotha. Those Christians of the future who are inspired and imbued by the Christ-Ego will also understand something that was formerly known to no one but the illuminates. Not only will they understand the Christ who has gone through death, but they will also understand the triumphant Christ of the Apocalypse, whose coming was previously prophesied and who arose from the dead into the spiritual fire. And Easter can always be to us a symbol of the risen Christ, a connecting link from the Christ on the cross to the triumphant, risen, elevated Christ who draws all human beings upward as He sits at the right side of the Father.

The Easter symbol opens a perspective not only on the future of the entire earth but also on that of human evolution. Easter is our assurance that some day the human beings inspired by Christ will increasingly change from Saul to Paul individuals and become more and more capable of seeing a spiritual fire. To be sure, just as Christ appeared to Moses and to those who had declared their faith in Him in the physical fire of the bramblebush and in the lightning on Sinai as a prophecy of His own coming, so will He appear to us in the spiritualized fire of the future. "He is with us every day to the end of the world," and to those who allowed their perception to be illuminated by the Event of Golgotha, to those He will appear in the spiritual fire even if at first they had seen Him in a different form.

Since Christ exerted such a profound influence on all aspects of earthly life, as far down as the human skeleton, that which formed His mortal body out of the elements of the earth also cleansed and sanctified all substances on the earth to such an extent that the world can never again become what the Wise Men of the East sadly feared it would forever be. They believed that the illuminate of the future, the Maitreya-Buddha, would be unable to find people on earth who could rise to an understanding of him because they would have sunk too deeply into the material world.

Christ was led to Golgotha to sublimate matter and redirect it to spiritual heights and to prevent fire on earth from becoming slag instead of spiritualized essence. When human beings themselves are spiritualized, they will again understand the primeval wisdom of the spiritual world from which they have formerly come. And thus, after human beings have gone through an even deeper understanding, the Maitreya-Buddha will find on earth an appreciation that otherwise he would have been unable to encounter. We understand everything that we learned in our youth better after we have become more mature through our trials and after we can look back upon the experiences of our youth. Similarly, mankind will understand the primeval wisdom of

115

the world by looking back at it in the light of Christ and through the Event of Golgotha.

And now, how can the imperishable remains of Kashyapa be saved, and for what destination are they being saved? It is written that the Maitreya-Buddha will appear and touch him with the right hand, and then the corpse will be removed in a fire. The fire that Paul saw on the way to Damascus was the same wonderful, spiritualized fire within which the body of Kashyapa will be safely transported upward; and in this fire everything great and noble of ancient times will be saved. We will see the forces of the past that were sublime, magnificent, and full of wisdom stream and flow into what humanity has gained as a result of the Mystery of Golgotha.

In the Easter bells, we encounter a symbol for the resurrection of the Earth Spirit itself and for the salvation of mankind. In the past, there has been no one with a proper understanding of this symbol who did not know how to elevate himself or herself to spiritual heights through the Easter mystery. It is not without significance that Faust, when he is near death, is tolled back into a new life by the Easter bells. This leads to the great moment in his old age when he ultimately becomes blind in the face of death and is able to say, "Yet inside me there shines a brilliant light."[39] Now he is ready to penetrate the spiritual worlds above where all noble members of mankind find salvation.

Everything that has once been alive in the past has been saved, purified, and sheltered in the etherealized spirituality that the Mystery of Golgotha diffused onto earth and into mankind. Some day when Maitreya-Buddha appears, the imperishable body of the great sage Kashyapa will undergo a similar purification in the wonderful fire, in the great light of Christ, that appeared to Paul on the way to Damascus.

Lecture IX
Ancient Revelation and Learning How to Ask Modern Questions
Kristiania (Oslo), May 16, 1909

Today we shall stress more the occult side of yesterday's observation. The four post-Atlantean cultures somehow had to reflect the great cosmic events in the souls of human beings as they had happened in historical sequence. However, beginning with the thirteenth or fourteenth century of our cultural epoch, such a reflection no longer took place because the external events in human evolution must be traced to more profound reasons.

We know that the etheric bodies of the great Atlantean initiates had been preserved for the Seven Holy Rishis, and we also know how the etheric and astral body of Zarathustra had been woven into those of Moses and Hermes. At any time the possibility existed that such etheric bodies, which had been cultivated and prepared by the initiates, could be further used in the spiritual economy of the world. But other things took place as well. For especially important personalities, such etheric bodies are formed in the higher worlds. When somebody was especially important for the mission of humanity, an etheric body or an astral body was woven in the higher worlds and was then imprinted on this personality.

This is what happened in the case of Shem who indeed has something to do with the whole tribe of the Semites. A

117

special etheric body was coined for such a tribal ancestor, and Shem became a sort of dual personality by this process. It may sound fantastic to the modern mind, but a clairvoyant would see a personality like Shem as he would see an ordinary human being with his or her aura; but then also in such a way as if a higher being that extends down from higher worlds completely filled his etheric body and as if the aura became a mediator between this personality and the higher world. Residing in a human being, such a divine being, however, has a very special power: it can multiply such an etheric body, and the multiplied etheric bodies then form a web that is continually woven into the descendants. Thus the descendants of Shem received an imprint of the copy of his etheric body. However, the Mystery Centers kept not only the multiplied copies but also the etheric body of Shem himself. Any personality that was meant to receive a special mission had to use this etheric body if it wanted to be able to communicate with the Semitic people, similar to the way in which a very educated European would have to learn the language of the Hottentots if he wanted to communicate with them. Therefore, the personality with a special mission had to bear within himself the real etheric body of Shem in order to be able to communicate with the Semitic people. Such a personality, for example, was Melchizedek: he could show himself to Abraham only in the etheric body of Shem.

We now have to ask ourselves something. If it is only now, in the fifth post-Atlantean cultural epoch, possible for us to develop an understanding for Christianity, what was the situation in the remainder of the Graeco-Latin era, which lasted into the thirteenth and fourteenth centuries? A mysterious, occult process took place. Christ lived only three years in the sheaths of Jesus of Nazareth, who was such a sublime individuality that He was able to leave the physical world at the age of thirty when the dove appeared over His head so that He could enter the spiritual world. Since the Christ-Individuality lived in the physical body, it filled out the three highly developed bodies of Jesus. Invisible to the physical eye, they were now multiplied as had formerly been the case with the etheric body of Shem so that the copies of the etheric and astral bodies of Jesus of Nazareth were available from the time he died on the cross. This has nothing to do with His ego; it passed into the spiritual world and has repeatedly reincarnated itself afterward.

We see how Christian writers in the first few centuries after the Christ-Event still worked on the basis of an oral tradition that was transmitted by the disciples of the Apostles, who set great value on a direct, physical transmission of the Christ-Event. However, this would not have been a sufficient building block for later centuries, and that is why a copy of the etheric body of Jesus of Nazareth was woven into especially eminent heralds of the Christian message beginning with the sixth and seventh centuries. One such herald was Augustine, who in his youth had to go through tremendous struggles. However, only when the impulse of the etheric body of Jesus of Nazareth came to work in him in a significant way did he begin to become engaged in Christian mysticism of his own initiative. His writings can be understood only in this light. Many other personalities in the world, such as Columban,[40] Gallus,[41] and Patrick,[42] carried within themselves such a copy of Jesus's etheric body and were therefore in a position to spread Christianity and built a bridge from the Christ-Event to the succeeding times.

By contrast, we see human beings whose astral body received the astral body of Jesus of Nazareth in the eleventh and twelfth centuries. Such a personality was Francis of Assisi. When we look at his life from this point of view, we will understand it in quite a few ways. His qualities of humility and Christian devotion will become especially clear to us when we tell ourselves that such a mystery lived in

119

him. In the time from about the eleventh through the thirteenth centuries such human beings became the heralds of Christianity by the very fact that the astral body of Jesus was woven into their own astral body. Hence, they received Christianity by virtue of Grace.

Although the ego of Jesus of Nazareth left its three sheaths at the baptism of John, a copy of this ego remained in each of them similar to the imprint a seal leaves behind. The Christ-Being took possession of these three bodies and of that which remained as the imprint of the Jesus-Ego. Beginning with the twelfth, thirteenth, and fourteenth centuries, something like an ego copy of Jesus was woven into human beings who began to speak of an "inner Christ." Meister Eckhart and Tauler were individuals who spoke from their own experience like an ego copy of Jesus of Nazareth.

There are still many people present who carry within themselves something like the various bodies of Jesus of Nazareth, but these are now no longer the leading personalities. Increasingly we can see how there are human beings in the fifth epoch who must rely on themselves and on their own ego and how such inspired people have become a rarity. It was therefore necessary that a spiritual tendency develop in our fifth epoch to ensure that humanity would continue to be imbued with spiritual knowledge. Those individualities who were capable of looking into the future had to take care that human beings in the times to come would not be left simply to rely on their human ego only. The legend of the Holy Grail relates that the chalice from which the Christ Jesus took the Last Supper with his disciples was kept in a certain place. We see in the story of Parsifal the course of a young person's education typical for our fifth post-Atlantean epoch. Parsifal had been instructed not to ask too many questions, and his dilemma arose from his following those instructions. That is the important transition from the traditional to more modern times: in ancient India and later with Augustine and Francis of Assisi the student had to live in a state of the highest degree of passive devotion. All these humble people allowed themselves to be inspired by what was already alive in them and by what had been woven into them. But now things changed in that the ego became a questioning ego. Today, any soul that accepts passively what is given to it cannot transcend itself because it merely oberves the happenings in the physical world around it. In our times the soul has to ask questions; it has to rise above itself; it has to grow beyond its given form. It must raise questions, just as Parsifal ultimately learned to inquire after the mysteries of the Grail's Castle.[43]

Spiritual investigation today begins only where there is questioning, and the souls today that are stimulated by external science to ask questions and to search are the Parsifal souls. And this has led to the introduction of Rosicrucian education—that much maligned mystery school of thought —that accepts tradition gratefully but does not accept traditional wisdom blindly. Yet that which today constitutes Rosicrucian spiritual orientation has been investigated in the higher worlds directly with the spiritual eye and with the means the student himself has been instructed to utilize. This has not come about simply because this or that is written in old books or because certain people believed one thing or another. Rather, the Rosicrucian spiritual method proclaims wisdom that has been investigated today. It was gradually prepared in the Rosicrucian schools that were founded in the thirteenth and fourteenth centuries as a result of the work of an individuality by the name of Christian Rosenkreutz.

This accumulated wisdom can today be proclaimed as Spiritual Science. This is so because today it is no longer possible to instill in human beings what is to inspire them from the inside without their having a hand in the process. Today people who feel that Spiritual Science speaks to their hearts must approach it through their own free will, through their own free impulse, and through the fact that they feel enlivened by spiritual knowledge. Hence we need not attempt to stir up an interest in Spiritual Science.

Through this theosophical-Rosicrucian orientation of the spirit, we again bring close to ourselves what is still present in the copies of Jesus of Nazareth's ego. Those who prepare themselves in this manner will pull into their souls the copy of the ego of Jesus of Nazareth so that they become like imprints of a seal, and it is in this way that the Christ-Principle finds its way into the human soul. Rosicrucianism prepared something positive, and since anthroposophy is meant to become life, the souls that absorb and truly accept it will gradually undergo a metamorphosis. To accept anthroposophy within yourself means to change the soul in such a way that it is able to come to a true understanding of the Christ.

The anthroposophist makes himself or herself a living recipient of what was given to Moses and Paul in the Javeh-Christ-Revelation. It is written in the fifth letter of the Apocalypse that the people in the fifth cultural epoch are those who can really absorb the things that will be quite obvious for the cultural period of the Philadelphia community. The wisdom of the fifth cultural period will open as a flower of love in the sixth period.

Today mankind is called upon to accept into itself something new, something divine, and thereby to undertake again the ascent into the spiritual world. The Spiritual Scientific teaching of evolution is being imparted not because people are supposed to put their blind faith into it, but because mankind is supposed to reach an understanding of it through its own powers of judgment. This teaching is being directed to those who bear the core of the Parsifal nature within themselves. And it is not being proclaimed just in special places or to a special group of people, but human beings from all of humanity will come together to listen to the call of spiritual wisdom.

Lecture X

The God of the Alpha and the God of the Omega

Berlin, May 25, 1909

It is often emphasized, and with good reason, that Spiritual Science should not simply be a theory about the world, life, and the human being, but that it should become the most profound content of the human soul: that which gives life its meaning. If one approaches Spiritual Science with the right attitude, it can indeed become the very substance of life within a human being. However, let me stress emphatically that it can take on this function only gradually, little by little, because Spiritual Science is much like everything that grows and develops: first it must have a seed that keeps growing, and then by virtue of this growth it becomes ever more effective.

It is also a fact that nobody could hope to extract from Spiritual Science the right way of life just by an intellectual understanding of its truths. Judging Spiritual Science by its outward features, one may come to the conclusion that it is a view of the world, albeit one that is more comprehensive and sublime than others. But no, it is still something else, for what other theory would be able to advance those comprehensive ideas about Saturn, Sun, and Moon? What other theories of the world today would dare to make very concise statements about this? None, because they end up with abstract concepts when they attempt to raise themselves above the objects we perceive with our physical eyes and

123

ears. Such theories and conceptions of the world can offer only vague concepts about the divine that weaves and works behind material reality. As far as other less ambitious truths are concerned, such as the doctrines of reincarnation and of karma, Spiritual Science is also far ahead of anything traditional science has to offer when it talks about the evolution of the human being. To be sure, science too could adopt these doctrines for if one really wants to draw the proper conclusions from the materialistic-scientific facts, reincarnation and karma would long have been popular ideas. However, because modern scientists have not dared to come to these conclusions, the discussion about the subject has simply been put to rest. Evolution from the perspective of natural history and of history is discussed, but nobody wants to hear anything of the true evolution of the human individuality, which continues from one life to another and carries the human soul into the future.

Those who observe life properly will be compelled by its very consequences to embrace the doctrine of the four members of the human constitution, which is also revealed by clairvoyant investigation. But because thinking in the modern age lacks all courage, this doctrine is proclaimed only by Spiritual Science, which as a body of knowledge is in many ways ahead of other conceptions of the world and of the philosophies presented to human beings at the present time.

However, when all has been said and done, all that is not the real fruit of Spiritual Science. Its fruit does not consist in the fact that one accepts its teaching as satisfying and far-reaching. We cannot have the fruit without the seed. What we develop today as the fruit of the anthroposophical world view can make our hearts happy and warm our capacity to love. Yet nobody can enjoy this fruit of our spiritual scientific world view without the seed, that is without spiritual scientific knowledge itself. People may say: Of what use are these ideas about reincarnation and karma, or about the members of the human constitution and the evolution of the world? What is really important is the development of human love and of moral character. To this I would answer: Certainly, that is important, but true human love that is fruitful for the world is possible only on the basis of knowledge—Spiritual Scientific knowledge.

As a branch of knowledge, Spiritual Science has an advantage over other world conceptions in many areas. When it is experienced by us in a truly intimate manner, when we do not tire to awaken in our souls time and again those great comprehensive thoughts and carry them with us, then we will see that this body of teaching can in a very definite sense become the content and substance of one's life. Spiritual scientific teaching is a body of ideas that leads us into supersensible worlds, and in spiritual scientific thinking we must therefore soar to higher worlds. Every hour spent in spiritual scientific study means that the soul reaches out beyond the concerns of everyday life. The moment we devotedly give ourselves to the teaching, we are transported into another world. Our ego is then united with the spiritual world out of which it was born. Thus, when we think in a spiritual scientific way, we are with our ego in our spiritual home, at the fountainhead from which it came.

If we understand this in the right sense, then we can truly compare spiritual scientific thinking with that state of consciousness that we recognize from the spiritual point of view as sleep. When human beings fall asleep at night and sleep themselves into a spiritual world, then they have transported the ego into the world whence it was born and from which it emerges every morning so that it can pass into the world of the senses within the human body. In times to come, the soul will live consciously within this spiritual world; however, at the present such is normally not the case. And why not? It is because in the course of the ages consciousness of the spiritual world has become weaker and weaker in the ego. In the Atlantean epoch the ego during sleep saw itself surrounded by divine-spiritual beings, but after the Atlantean catastrophe the ego was pushed out into the world of the senses and increasingly lost its capacity to gaze into the world that it inhabits during sleep. The idea that the ego is blotted out at night and resurrected in the morning is absurd. It is in the spiritual world but is not conscious of it.

Spiritual scientific thinking gives us the strength to tie ourselves consciously, little by little, to these spiritual realities. By leading us—at least in thinking—into the spiritual world, anthroposophy has certain beneficial qualities in common with sleep. The cares and worries that issue from the things of the sense world are obliterated in sleep. If human beings are able to sleep and their thinking is blotted out, they forget all worries. That is the most beneficent effect of sleep, an effect resulting from the fact that the ego lets the forces of the spiritual world stream into it during sleep. These spiritual streams contain strengthening forces, the effect of which is to help us forget our worries and cares during sleep and also to repair the damage that such worries and cares have inflicted upon our organism. The injuries caused by the sense world are healed by spiritual powers— hence the refreshment, the regeneration that every healthy sleep bestows upon us. In a higher sense, these then are the qualities that spiritual scientific thinking has in common with sleep.

Spiritual thoughts are powerful if we accept them as living forces. When we elevate ourselves to the thoughts that are connected with the past and the future of the earth and allow these momentous events to work on us, then our keyed-up soul will be drawn to these events, far away from the worries of the day. Thoughts of how the ideal of our own sovereign will grows for us out of karma—this plan of destiny—give us courage and strength so that we say to ourselves: "However insurmountable some of the problems of

126

our lives may be today, our strength will grow from one incarnation to the next. The sovereign will within us is becoming stronger every day, and all the obstacles will help us to strengthen it even more. In the process of overcoming these obstacles, our will is going to develop ever more, and our energy is going to increase. The trivialities of life, all the inferior things in our existence, will melt away as the hoar does in the sun—melted by the very sun that rises in the wisdom that permeates our spiritual thinking. Our world of feeling is made to glow throughout and becomes warm and transillumined; our whole existence will be broadened, and we will feel happy in it.''

When such moments of inner activity are repeated and we allow them to work on us, a strengthening of our whole existence into all directions will emanate from this process. Not from one day to the next, to be sure, but constant repetition of such thoughts will bring about the gradual disappearance of our depressions, lamentations about our fate, and an excessively melancholy temperament. Spirit knowledge will be medicine for our soul, and when that happens, the horizon of our existence widens and implants in us that way of thinking that is the fruit of all spirit knowledge. This resulting way of thinking and feeling, this attitude of mind and heart, must be considered the ideal state to which spiritual scientific endeavors can lead. All discord, all disharmonies of life will disappear opposite the harmonious thoughts and feelings that bring about an energetic will. Thus, spiritual investigation proves to be not just knowledge and doctrine, but also a force of life and a substance of our soul. Seen in this light, Spiritual Science is capable of working in life in such a way that it frees human beings from cares and worries. And that is how it has to work in our time, for it owes its existence not to arbitrariness, but to the knowledge that it is needed.

The individualities who in their knowledge were far

ahead of normal human beings, the Masters of Wisdom and of the Harmony of Feelings, knew that Spiritual Science had to flow into our culture if it was not to wither. Spiritual Science is a new sap of life, and humanity needs such new sap from time to time. Spiritual Science is the stream necessary for our time. Those who have a feeling for these great truths should hurry to us and absorb the truths so that they can be salt and ferment for the spiritual life of all humanity. The striving individual must see this as a sort of duty. It is not difficult to understand why the highest authorities have issued a call for Spiritual Science in our time precisely so that those with open hearts and unprejudiced minds may be assembled.

We have been viewing with our souls post-Atlantean humanity and have traced its cultural epochs from the ancient Indian down to our own fifth post-Atlantean epoch. We have seen that during this time human beings lost their consciousness of the spiritual world bit by bit. In the first epoch, the ancient Indian, human beings still had a profound yearning for the spiritual world. The world of the senses was considered *maya*, illusion. Then came the ages that issued a call to human beings to do external, physical labor. Human beings had to learn to love the world of the senses because only then were they able to cultivate it. At this time, human beings no longer said that the external world was nothing but *maya*. On the contrary, human beings now had to immerse themselves into the world and work on it with their faculties and wisdom. That, however, resulted in human beings' gradually losing the consciousness of the spiritual world so that Zarathustra, the initiator of the Persian culture, felt compelled to tell his disciples: "All living beings are called into existence by the force that streams from the sun as physical force. But this physical force is not the only thing. In the sun lives Ahura Mazdao—the spiritual Sun Being." It was necessary to demonstrate to people how

128

the material world is but the physical expression of the spiritual world.

Thus it was first in the ancient Persian epoch that there arose the sentiment that would express itself as follows: "Certainly, what the sun shines upon is *maya*, but I must seek the spirit behind this *maya*. The spiritual world is always around me, but I cannot experience it with physical eyes and ears. I can experience it only with supersensible consciousness. Once this consciousness has been awakened, then in the physical existence also can I recognize the Great Spirit of the Sun with all its subordinate beings who also belong to the Sun. But an age is approaching when my soul will no longer have this knowledge." It was difficult to transmit this knowledge fully to human beings. They must gradually be made more mature through renewed incarnations in order to recognize the divine-spiritual element behind all physical phenomena and to understand that all of nature is permeated by it.

In the ancient Persian culture, human beings were still capable of recognizing the divine element in this life, but they were unable to take this consciousness into the time period between death and rebirth. For the peculiar thing in this epoch was that consciousness between death and rebirth became increasingly darker. By contrast, let us look at the soul of an individual in ancient India. When it passed through death into the other world, it lived there among spiritual beings in a comparatively light-filled world. In the Persian culture, such was less the case; the world between death and rebirth had become darker. Obstacles between various souls accumulated, and the soul felt lonely; in a manner of speaking, it could not extend its hand to another soul. But that is the difficult and dark side of life in the spiritual world: the soul may not share its path with others.

In the Egyptian epoch, a substantial part of the soul's capacity to link up with other souls had already been lost to such an extent that the soul longed for the preservation of the physical body, which was to be preserved in the mummy. The reason for this was that the soul sensed it had very little strength that could be taken into the life between death and rebirth. Human beings at this time wanted to preserve the physical body so that the soul might be able to look down on it as on something that belonged to it, thus compensating for the power it no longer had in the spiritual world. Cultural phenomena such as mummification are deeply connected with the evolution of the human soul.

An Egyptian had the notion that in death he would be united with Osiris. He said these words to himself: "Long ago, in ancient ages, the soul was able to gaze into the beyond. It has now lost this visionary power, but it can make up for the loss if in this life it develops qualities by which it will become more and more like Osiris himself. The soul will then itself become Osiris-like and will be united with Osiris after death." And so, by clinging to Osiris, the soul tried to create a surrogate for everything that could no longer be preserved from ancient times.

However, what Osiris was unable to give to the human soul is told in an Egyptian legend, whereby Osiris was once living with human beings on earth, until his evil brother Seth shut him up in a wooden box similar to a casket. This means that Osiris did live on earth with human beings when they were still more spiritual. But then he had to remain in the spiritual world because he was too sublime to fit into the physical human form. Similarly, if the soul wanted to create a substitute for the lost spiritual power of vision between death and rebirth, it had to become a being that is too sublime, too good for the human form. By becoming similar to Osiris, the soul would be able to overcome its loneliness in the beyond, but it could not take into a new incarnation what it had received in the spiritual world through the characteristics it had in common with Osiris. This is so because, after all, Osiris was not suited for this physical incarnation.

The grave danger threatening humankind in those times was that incarnations were steadily deteriorating because there could be no new influx of spiritual forces. Only what had remained from ancient ages could be further developed, and all that reached its ultimate maturity in Graeco-Roman times. This was made manifest in the magnificent art of the Greeks—the mature fruit from earlier blossoms. Greek art was the finest fruit of the heritage bequeathed to humanity beginning with primeval times. But hand in hand with this accomplishment came the feeling of deep darkness in the life between death and new birth, and a noble Greek individual was right when he said: "Better to be a beggar in the upper world than a king in the realm of the shadows."[44] Yes indeed, human beings in Greece and the Roman states possessed so much to delight and satisfy their senses, but they could take nothing with them into the life between death and new birth.

Then came the event of Golgotha—the event that is of significance not only for the external physical world, but also for all the worlds through which a human being must pass. The moment when the blood flowed from the wounds of the Redeemer, when the corpse was hanging on the cross, the Christ appeared in the underworld and kindled the light that once again gave sight to the souls below. And the soul was able to realize from that moment on that once again strength could also be derived from the world below and benefit the physical world. No longer does the soul endeavor to unite itself with Osiris in order to have a surrogate for the loss of vision. From now on, it could say to itself: "In the underworld, too, I can find the light of Christ—that which has immersed itself into the earth, for the Christ has become the spirit of the earth. And now I imbibe a new force from a spiritual fountainhead, a force that I can take back to earth when I return for a new incarnation.

131

What was necessary so that this force could flow into the soul in the right way? A complete reversal in the way human beings looked at the physical world was necessary. First, let us ask what the people in ancient India experienced when we reconstruct what one of them might have said: "This world is *maya*, the great illusion. Whenever I perceive this world and relate myself to it, I have fallen victim to the illusion. Only by withdrawing from it and by elevating myself to primeval spiritual things beyond the world of the senses can I be in the world of the gods. Only by withdrawing from the outer world can I traverse through my inner being that has remained with me as an ancient legacy of these spiritual worlds and thus return to my ancient home. I must return to this primeval holy realm from which I once started out to the world of the senses, and I can return only by giving free rein to my spiritual powers, thereby diverting my attention from the lure of the outer world." In the days of the ancient Indian culture it was possible for human beings to take this step back into the far-distant past. Inside of them, they had retained much of the force that could help an individual, if properly applied, to find the way back to the old gods. Thus did the human being in ancient India find his *Devas*, the beings from whom everything had come into existence.

Now came the epoch of ancient Persia, when the human soul had lost much of the power that was like a legacy from ancient times. If in this epoch the soul had said: "I will turn back because I do not wish to remain in this world," it would not have found the ancient gods because the power to make that possible was no longer adequate. This fact is related to the evolution of humanity. Had the soul attempted to divert its gaze away from the outer world and consider it as nothing but *maya*, this would have led to its seeing not the higher gods, but rather the subordinate *Devas* who were evil spiritual beings that did not belong to the ranks of higher gods. Because this danger existed, the soul had to be shown how this world of the senses could be seen as the outward expression of the spiritual by starting from the world of the senses and not turning away from it. In looking up to the sun, the soul learned to see in it not only its external physical sun force, but also the Sun God Ahura Mazdao, and thereby it learned to know something of the divine-spiritual reality.

The soul of the ancient Persian had become too weak to activate the spiritual forces that could lead it back to the ancient gods. Hence, it had to be educated to pierce through the veil of materiality covering the spiritual. In the outer world the evil Asuras lay hidden, but human beings were not yet capable of seeing the beneficent spiritual beings beyond the world that was regarded as *maya*. That is why all names for spiritual beings came to be reversed during the time between the Indian and the Persian epochs. Devas were the good beings in ancient India, but in the Persian culture, they became the evil gods. The true reason for this reversal is evident from the continuing development of the human soul; in relation to the external world it had become increasingly stronger, in relationship to the inner world, increasingly weaker.

Preparation for what was to come was now made by those beings who guide and direct human evolution. After Zarathustra had learned to look up to the sun and see in its aura the Sun God, he knew that this Sun God was no one else but the Christ-Spirit, who at that time could reveal Himself only from outside the world. The human being in his soul here on earth could not yet perceive the Christ-Being. The being that was formerly seen in the sun and had been given the name Ahura Mazdao had to descend to earth because only then could the human being learn from within to recognize a *Deva*, a divinely spiritual principle, within his own soul. In the age of ancient Persia, life in the human body was not yet capable of receiving the Christ-Spirit, let alone be permeated by it. All that had to happen slowly and gradually. We must acquaint ourselves with the thought that the gods can reveal themselves only to those who prepare themselves as recipients of a revelation. *Deva*, the god who can be perceived through our inner forces, could appear only to that part of humanity that had prepared itself for his coming.

Everything in human evolution comes to pass slowly and gradually, and evolution does not proceed everywhere in the same manner. After the Atlantean flood, the tribes had migrated to the East. Since they settled in various regions, their development also differed. What enabled the ancient Indian to have a vivid feeling for the spiritual world? This happened because the evolution of the ego in this part of the world had taken a very special course. In the people of ancient India the ego had remained deeply entrenched in the spiritual world so that it was disinclined to make much contact with the physical world. It was the peculiar characteristic of an individual in ancient India that he or she would cling to the spirituality of preceding ages while at the same time confining relations with the physical world to a minimum. Since the individual in ancient India did not want to connect his or her ego with the physical world, the achievements of external civilization have not blossomed in India or in many other regions of the East where people by and large seem to have lacked inventive genius. By contrast, the inventiveness of the people in the West prompted them to take hold of the external world since they considered it their task to cultivate and improve it. Ancient Persia formed, as it were, the boundary between East and West. The people who paid little attention to the material existence in this world tended to settle and remain in the East. That is why the teaching of a Buddha was still necessary for the people of the East six hundred years before Christ. Buddha had to be placed into world evolution at this juncture because it was his mission to keep alive in the souls the longing for the spiritual worlds of the past, and that is why he had to preach against the thirst for entering the physical world. However, he was preaching at a time when the soul still had the inclination, but no longer the capacity, to elevate itself into the spiritual worlds. Buddha preached to human beings the sublime truths about suffering, and he brought to them the insights that could lift the soul above this world of suffering.

Such teaching would have been unsuitable for the Western world. It needed a doctrine that was in tune with the people's inclination to embrace the physical world and that could be summarized by the following explanation: "You must work in the outer world in such a way that the forces of this world are placed in the service of humanity; but after death, you can also take the fruits of your life into the spiritual world."

The peculiar essence of Christianity is usually not properly understood. In the Roman world it did not appeal much to those who were able to enjoy the treasures and riches of this world, but those who were condemned to toil in the physical world liked Christianity. They knew that in spite of all their work in the physical world, they were developing something in this life that they could take with them after death. Such was the feeling of exaltation inspiring the souls of those who accepted Christianity. Human beings could say to themselves: "By setting up Christ as my ideal, I develop something in this world that cannot be annihilated even by death." This consciousness could develop only because Christ had actually been on earth not as a *Deva*, but as a being who had incarnated in a human body and who could be a model and an ideal for every human being. For this to happen, the impulse and the proper forces had to be created, and this preparatory work had been done by Zarathustra. He had experienced so much that he was prepared to take this mission.

In ancient Persia, Zarathustra had been able to behold

the Sun God in the aura of the sun, but he had had to prepare himself for that task in earlier incarnations. During the era that was still inspired by the teachings of the Holy Rishis, Zarathustra had already gone through some sublime experiences in incarnations. He had been initiated into the teachings of the Holy Rishis, having absorbed them stage by stage in seven subsequent incarnations. Then he was born into a body that was blind and deaf, which afforded him as little contact with the outer world as was possible. Zarathustra had to be born as a human being who was practically nonsusceptible to outer sense impressions, and then out of his innermost being the memory of the teachings of the Holy Rishis from a previous incarnation welled up in him. And at that moment the Great Sun God was able to kindle in him something that went ever further than the wisdom received from the Holy Rishis. That experience awakened in him again in his next incarnation, and it was then that Ahura Mazdao revealed himself to Zarathustra from without.

You can see, therefore, that Zarathustra had experienced a great deal before he could become the teacher and inspirer of the people of ancient Persia. We also know that Moses and Hermes were his disciples and that he gave his astral body to Hermes and his etheric body to Moses. Moses was the first to proclaim the teaching that emanated from the Akasha Chronicle, the teaching of the "*I am the I am.*" (*Ejeh asher ejeh*). And thus Zarathustra prepared himself slowly for an even greater and more prodigious sacrifice. When Zarathustra's astral body reappeared in Hermes and his etheric body in Moses, his ego—whose development had steadily progressed—was able to form a new astral body and a new etheric body for the new incarnation, commensurate with the full powers of the ego. And six hundred years before Christ, Zarathustra was born again in the land of Chaldaea and became the teacher of Pythagoras under the name Zarathos, or Nazarathos. Within the Chaldaean culture he then prepared the new impulse that was to come into the world. This is reflected in that passage of the New Testament that speaks of the Three Wise Men from the East who came to greet the Christ as the new Star of Wisdom. Zarathustra had taught that the Christ would come, and those who were left as disciples of this significant Zarathustra doctrine knew at what point in time the great Impulse of Golgotha would arrive.

There is always a certain connection between great individualities of the world, such as Buddha, Zarathustra, and Pythagoras, because what is at work in the world is a force—a fact. Great spirits work together, and they are born into a certain age for a purpose. Likewise, the great impulses in human evolution weave themselves into each other. Zarathustra had pointed to the One who was to make it possible, through the Event of Golgotha, for human beings to find the world of the *Devas* through the force of their own inner being; moreover, they would be increasingly able to do so as they developed forward into the future. And in the same epoch, the Buddha was teaching: Yes, there is a spiritual world, compared to which the whole world of the senses is *maya*. Turn your steps back into the world in which you were before the thirst for an earthly existence awakened, and then you will find Nirvana—rest within the divine!

Such is the difference between the teachings of Buddha and Zarathustra. Buddha taught that the human being can reach the divine by going back; Zarathustra, in his incarnation as Zarastra, taught that the time is approaching when the light will incarnate within the earth itself, which will enable the progressive soul to come closer to the divine. Buddha said, the soul would find God by going back; Zarathustra said it would find Him by going forward.

Regardless of whether you regress or progress, whether you seek God in the Alpha or in the Omega, you will be able to find Him. What is important is that you find Him with

137

your own heightened human power. Those forces necessary to find the God of the Alpha are the primal forces of a human being. However, the forces necessary to find the God of the Omega must be acquired here on earth by striving human beings themselves. It makes a difference whether one goes back to Alpha or forward to Omega. He who is content with finding God and just wants to get into the spiritual world has the choice of going forward or backward. However, the individual who is concerned that humanity leave the earth in a heightened state must point the way to Omega—as did Zarathustra.

Zarathustra prepared the way for that part of humanity that was to become involved with the very forces of the earth. Yet Zarathustra also fully understood the Buddha, for their quest was ultimately the same. What was Zarathustra's task? He had to make it possible for the Christ-Impulse to descend to the earth. Zarathustra was reborn as Jesus of Nazareth, and because of what had transpired in the previous incarnation, his individuality was able to unite itself with many a force that had been preserved as a result of spiritual economy. The world is profound and truth is complicated!

There was also interwoven in Jesus of Nazareth the being of the Buddha. It had advanced on different paths because many powers work in the one who is supposed to have an influence on humankind. The ego of Jesus left the physical, etheric, and astral bodies at baptism in the Jordan River, and the Sun God—the Christ-Spirit—entered and lived three years in the bodies of Jesus of Nazareth. And this is how Zarathustra had prepared humanity to be the recipient of the Christ-Impulse.

An important moment in the evolution of the earth had arrived with these events. It had now become possible for human beings to find God in their innermost being; in addition, they were now able to take something with them from the life between death and new birth into the new incarnation. And now, in our own age, there are already present souls who feel strongly enough that they have been in a world illumined by the Light of Christ. The fact that this is dimly divined in many a soul means that human beings today are capable of receiving and understanding the teachings of Spiritual Science. And because such people exist today, the Masters of Wisdom and of the Harmony of Feelings have expressed the hope that such people will also feel the truths of Spiritual Science and will make them the very substance of their lives. Knowing all this, the Masters assigned the mission of proclaiming anthroposophy in the present age to those who have already attained a high level of understanding.

It is essential that Spiritual Science begin now to become a spiritual impulse of our time. Christ Himself has prepared human souls for Spiritual Science, and it is guaranteed to stay in this world for the simple reason that the Light of Christ, once kindled, can never be extinguished. Once we inspire ourselves with the feeling that the stream of anthroposophical spirituality is a necessity, then we are immersed in it in the right way, and it will always stand before us as an unshakable ideal.

Yes, the human personality had to develop to such an extent that light could descend and say in a human body: "I am the Light of the world!" The Light of the World first came down into the soul of Zarathustra and spoke to it. Zarathustra's soul understood the meaning of this universal light and sacrificed itself so that these significant words would go out to all humanity—from a human body: "I am the Light of the World."

Lecture XI

From Buddha to Christ

A Lecture Given at the International Congress of
the Federation of European Sections of the
Theosophical Society

Budapest, May 31, 1909

I do not wish to offer you here an observation about the philosophy of religion or a treatise on literary history, nor do I wish to give you a scientific lecture about the subject matter. I simply want to tell you what Spiritual Science or occultism have to say about such great individualities as Buddha and Christ, more precisely what knowledge they can offer from the vantage point of Rosicrucian occultism.

In a lecture intended for more advanced theosophists, I presume you will permit me to speak more intimately of such truths. I shall present to you broad outlines, and I will incorporate certain details into them. Rosicrucian occultism presents one of the great principles of occult theosophical investigation from which spiritual life should flow into our hearts. Even though the goals and ideals of theosophy can also be found outside the Theosophical Society, there is nevertheless a difference in the means employed by anyone seriously trying to struggle for the attainment and right application of knowledge and truth, for occult investigation can and must flow directly into life.

Allow me to illustrate this point with a trivial example. The human soul is like a stove that does not need to be persuaded to heat a room because heating is its function. The stove does this on its own, provided we put wood into it and light it. It could be objected that the appearance of the wood does not suggest to us that it can generate heat, and yet it does precisely that. By putting some firewood, the appearance of which is so different from the stove, into it and lighting it, we bring warmth into our house. Similarly, by getting used to spiritual scientific concepts, we also become accustomed to our ability to make judgments and to orient ourselves freely in this world. It is not our task to preach ideals but rather to provide human souls with the fuel that can generate spiritual wisdom, genuine brotherliness, and true humanity. To realize this is our goal.

What we designate as the Rosicrucian stream arose in the thirteenth and fourteenth centuries when the spiritual stream of Christianity was already obscured since it had taken on an external form. At a time when Christianity in the outer world increasingly was taking on an external form and when its true original meaning had faded, Rosicrucianism, received the task to cultivate ancient wisdom and to preserve the treasures of primordial wisdom. In the outside world, wherever people deemed only external forms and hardened dogmas to be important, they abjured and cursed anything that was venerated in the mysteries as the highest and holiest truths. One frequently heard the words: "I curse Skythianos; I curse Boddha; I curse Zarathas." These are the three names that were venerated in greatest secrecy in the mysteries and in the Rosicrucian mystery schools as sacred names of the masters.

Zarathas is the same individual as Zarathustra—not the Zarathustra known to history, but the exalted individual who founded ancient Persian culture and who was the teacher in the occult schools of that time. Skythianos was a highly developed individual of ancient times. In one of his subsequent incarnations he led the occult schools of Central Asia,

141

and later he also became the teacher of esoteric schools in Europe. Boddha and Buddha are one and the same person.

In order to understand what an initiate felt when he heard these three names and in order to gain some idea of what they could give him, we have to go back in human evolution and examine the character of Rosicrucian occultism more closely. Let us gain an understanding through listening and through looking back into the past. There have always been highly advanced personalities who stood out from the masses and to whom average people looked up in reverence as one would to high ideals. To look up to the individuals who had reached such a lofty stage of wisdom and intellectual power had the effect of animating the average person's moral sense and vital energies. Even today the forces of these lofty spirits flow into our finer bodies.

Let us look back into the past to all the spiritual individualities of whom I want to speak to you, all the way back to the ancient Indian culture. If we went further back in human evolution to the remote age of Atlantis and its end, this would lead us to the event that separates us from an even more ancient epoch of humanity where our souls led lives greatly different from the ones they lead in our present physical bodies. However, rather than dealing in detail with a description of life and culture in those ancient times, let us today be content to illuminate the answer to the question: How was humanity guided in ancient times, and where did the forces that influenced it come from?

When a seer whose spiritual eye is opened so that he knows how to read the fine script of the Akasha Chronicle looks back into the spiritual worlds, he discovers the sites from which the culture and all spiritual life of those times emanated. Our souls can discover the sites where the masters and their disciples assembled in the mystery schools of that time. There were many such Mystery Centers on the ancient Atlantean continent, and they differed from those of today and were given a different name. They were not just churches and not just schools, but rather a combination of both. Those who searched for truth could find both religion and wisdom in the mystery schools; here, religion and wisdom were one. Using a modern word, we can characterize the concept of those cultic centers, the mystery schools, by the term "Atlantean Oracles." This is the name given to them by the European mystery schools, but originally they were called something entirely different.

In the Atlantean Oracles and their centers of wisdom, spiritual life was differentiated in the same way that external knowledge and the areas of trade and professions are subdivided in external life today. There were various branches of spiritual investigation and occult wisdom in ancient Atlantis, but everything in those times depended on different conditions. Wisdom varied from one oracle to another according to the capacities of the human beings and their external environment. A connection existed between certain human capacities and certain planets, that is, certain mystical occult capacities were connected with special planets. Therefore, on the Atlantean continent we should distinguish between oracles of the Moon, Mercury, Venus, Sun, Mars, Jupiter, and Saturn.

Our present capacities, too, developed out of the cosmos, as did our earth, and they are in each case tied to different planets and their influences. On Atlantis, people who were suited to develop this or that cognitive capacity were chosen from the population and assigned to one of the seven oracles. Of the seven oracles, which were named after the seven planets in ancient Atlantis, the Sun Oracle stood out from all the others, but next to it the Vulcan Oracle prepared itself in secrecy for its future task.

Each of these oracles had emanated from the cosmos according to its capacity, but there was one center in which the capacities of all seven oracles flowed together, and it was

143

here that the wisdom of the seven oracles in Atlantis coalesced. The adepts of this center, of the Holy Sun Oracle, had been initiated into the mystery and service of what we today know as the Sun. We should not forget that the physical sun is only the external expression or physiognomy—the body and garment—of the spiritual life of the exalted Sun-Being.

All of you have heard of the time when the sun separated from the earth, and along with the physical sun those beings abandoned the earthly arena who had advanced through the human state and, therefore, could no longer use the earth for their development. After the moon too had left, the earth was able to realize its destination of becoming the abode of humanity. If the sun alone had influenced the earth, the latter would have gone through such a rapid development that human beings would have become old soon after birth. By contrast, if our earth had been only under the influence of the moon, human beings would have been stiffened and become mummies. Development would have been too slow, and their bodies would have reached a state of rigidity and lignification. However, through a wise guiding force, sun and moon maintained a balance in the external influence they exert on the earth; and this enabled earth and human beings to develop at a speed suitable to them. The beings of Mars, Mercury, Venus, and so on, who did not need the forces that had left with the moon and earth for their development, departed with the sun to take up their own abode. Yet they continued to be connected with the earth and sent their beneficial forces down to it in the sunlight.

During the ancient Atlantean epoch, the adepts of the Sun Oracle had been initiated into the deeds of this lofty Sun-Being. The Great Initiate who was the leader of this highest oracle had been initiated in the most comprehensive ways into these mysteries. The entire ancient Atlantean and, as we shall see, also the post-Atlantean culture proceeded from him. The "Manu," as this leader of the Sun

Oracle was called—although the name doesn't really matter all that much—did not choose the main representatives of the post-Atlantean culture from among the so-called scholars and scientists, nor from the clairvoyants and Magi of that time. The people who were endowed with spiritual and psychic knowledge and who in those days were approximately comparable to the scientists and scholars of our time were not considered suitable by him; rather plain people who had begun gradually to lose the clairvoyant faculty were chosen. Our present state of consciousness began to develop only at the end of the Atlantean epoch. That was the time when the old clairvoyant consciousness was waning, gradually giving way to a full consciousness of self, to the ability to address the "I" in oneself. The great Manu gathered about him those who were able to function intellectually, not the clairvoyants and Magi but those who absorbed and developed the rudiments of arithmetic. They were the despised who knew nothing in the opinion of the leading people, and in this they were not unlike the theosophists today. Yet it was they with whom the great Manu journeyed to the sanctuary in Asia from which the post-Atlantean culture was to emanate.

Disregarding America for this purpose, let us say that Europe, Asia, and Africa have all been populated by the descendants of the ancient Atlanteans who had moved to these continents under Manu's leadership. This initiate of the Sun Oracle now had to take care that the founding of this post-Atlantean culture and the evolution of its human beings would proceed under the proper influence. From the very beginning he had to take care that everything that was valuable for a future development should be carried forward. This preservation of values from the past is a law of occultism, of spiritual economy, but it is also a law that can only be known through spiritual wisdom.

Now the Great Initiate took something very valuable

with him when he journeyed from ancient Atlantis to Europe. To accomplish this, he had—let me put it this way —traveled to and inspected the other oracles. You all know that in the case of ordinary people the etheric body separates from the astral body and the ego soon after death and gradually dissolves in the universal ether. The same happens with the astral body after a certain time, but this law is sometimes broken in the interest of spiritual economy. This is what happened in the case of the etheric bodies of the seven greatest initiates who were the leaders of the ancient Atlantean oracles.

What does it mean when we say we work on ourselves? It means that we purify the etheric body and the astral body. Now, once purified, the spiritualized etheric and astral bodies do not dissolve after death but are preserved in accordance with the law of spiritual economy. In short, it was known in the mysteries how to preserve the valuable etheric and astral bodies developed by the great initiates, but it would lead me too far afield to speak about this in detail. Suffice it to say that these bodies were kept by the preservers of the mystery schools.

It is for this reason that the Great Initiate of the Sun Oracle journeyed to the other Atlantean oracles to collect and take with him the seven etheric bodies of the greatest Atlantean initiates. And then he attracted through his wisdom a number of human beings who were to become fit for their coming culture. He taught these humans who were gathered around him so that they became increasingly more capable and pure. What followed may be called an art. After some time had elapsed, it became possible to incorporate the seven more important etheric bodies of the seven greatest initiates of the ancient Atlantean oracles into seven human beings. In regard to their egos, their power of judgment, and so on, they were simple people whose existence had no significance from an external point of view. However, they carried within them the seven most highly developed etheric bodies of the seven most significant initiates. These etheric bodies had streamed into these people, thereby enabling them to exude the great, powerful visions and truths of evolution through inspiration from above. Thus, they were able to speak of all this exalted wisdom.

The Great Initiate sent these seven bearers of wisdom to India where people still had a sense and an understanding of the spiritual and of spiritual worlds. In India human beings still had the feeling and the consciousness of having at one time emanated from a primordial spiritual world and of having been born from the womb of the Godhead. Therefore, the whole physical world appeared to them as *maya*, as illusion, and they longed to return to this world of the gods, to those divine-spiritual beings with whom they had once lived. To such people the seven bearers of wisdom could speak. They were called the Holy Rishis, and it was they who inaugurated the dawn of our post-Atlantean culture. The people who had preserved for themselves the consciousness of and the longing for the spiritual world with its divine-spiritual beings were thus given the opportunity to learn more about this world and to find the way back to it.

Subsequent ages gave birth to not only peoples who were destined to look into the spiritual worlds, but also to those who wanted to contribute to the founding of a new culture. They were meant to become fond of the physical world and to see it not only as *maya* or illusion. Rather, they began to understand that this physical world is but the expression or physiognomy of the spiritual world that lies behind it. This was the second epoch, the ancient Persian or Zarathustran culture. Ordinary history records only a relatively late Zarathustra because historians are unaware that it was customary in ancient times for a successor to receive the name of a great leader from the past. I am here referring to the greatest of all Zarathustras, who was one of the most intimate disciples of the Initiate of the Sun Oracle. His task was to find the connection between the physical and the spiritual world. He had to teach his disciples that the physical sphere of the sun is the body of spiritual beings who have their abode on the sun and that this whole physical world should be viewed as the members and limbs of the physical body of divine-spiritual beings. Just as the sun is surrounded by a great aura, so the human being is surrounded by his or her own small aura, which is a microcosmic expression of the sun's great aura. The sun is the body of the Sun Spirit who revealed himself in the Sun Oracle of the ancient Atlantean epoch. Zarathustra beheld this spirit in clairvoyant vision. He also designated the aura of the sun as Sun Spirit, and this is the same being whom he also called Ahura Mazdao. Occultists of later ages called it Ormuzd.

Zarathustra taught his disciples to see Ahura Mazdao in the physical sun and not to be led astray by Ahriman. Ahriman has lived in the physical world since the last third of the Atlantean epoch and attacks the human soul through sense perception, that is to say from the outside. By contrast, Lucifer attacks the soul from within. Zarathustra had to kindle in the hearts of humans the love for the great Sun Spirit, and he did this in powerful words that cannot be adequately rendered in our modern languages. All the magnificent words that you find in the Vedas and Gathas, no matter how beautiful, are but a feeble superficial expression of the great and lofty words originally uttered by Zarathustra. In our language, they can be approximated by the following:

"I wish to speak, now hearken and listen to me, you from near and from afar, who are filled with longing for these words. I want to speak about that which is the highest truth to me in this world and what was revealed to me by the great and mighty Ahura Mazdao. Hearken and listen to me now and mark my words carefully: No longer shall the teacher of falsehoods, the evil one whose lips bore witness to an evil faith, lead you astray for He—the mighty Ahura Mazdao—has manifested himself! Those who do not want to listen to the words as I say them and to the meaning that I give to them will experience evil things when the course of time reaches its end.''

And at other times Zarathustra said this: ''So great and mighty is He who revealed Himself to me in the sun that I surrender everything for him. I rejoice in sacrificing to Him the life of my body, the etheric existence of my senses, and the expression of my deeds''—the astral body. Such was the vow that Zarathustra made a long time ago.

Zarathustra had two disciples. To one of them he revealed through spiritual means everything that one can perceive with clairvoyant astral organs. This disciple was reincarnated under the name Hermes, the Egyptian Hermes. To the second disciple he imparted truths that one can know through the clairvoyant etheric body: the wisdom of the Akasha Chronicle. This second disciple was Moses, and you can find the wisdom imparted to him in the Book of Moses of the Old Testament.

When the first disciple was reincarnated as Hermes, he bore within him the astral body of Zarathustra, who had revealed to him not only his teachings, but also his own nature. Such a transfer is possible for what Hermes had received was nothing else but the astral body Zarathustra had sacrificed for him. Hence it was Zarathustra's wisdom that Hermes, the founder of the third post-Atlantean epoch, proclaimed.

The other disciple, to whom Zarathustra had given wisdom through the etheric body, was also born again. When he reincarnated, the etheric body that Zarathustra had sacrificed was woven into him. This disciple was Moses. You can find such facts recorded in religious documents, but in a veiled manner only. Read the story of the birth of Moses. What happened then? The child was placed into an ark of bulrushes which was then put into the water. What does that mean? It means that he was completely cut off from the world. His ego and astral body were not to become manifest until they were permeated by the principle of the etheric body. How can this take place? During the time when Moses lay isolated in the ark on the water, the etheric body that had been woven into him became illuminated. Only then could the astral body and the ego begin to work in him. Are not the powerful images of Genesis, which will occupy humanity for a long time to come, images taken from the Akasha Chronicle? These things cannot be understood without the aid of occultism.

We now come to the fourth epoch of the post-Atlantean culture, to the Graeco-Roman epoch. Up to this point, human beings were developed in such a way that they should learn to love the earth. Yet there were also those who had been the companions of the gods in the Atlantean age, and it is therefore justified to ask what had become of the egos of the great initiates of that time. Atlantean egos had dwelled in a softer and finer body, and for them existence on earth was such that individualities had to go through an incarnation only for the time necessary to maintain the connection between the world's primordial spiritual wisdom and humanity.

The great Buddha is one of the individualities who was actually able to imbue the oriental writings with that deep wisdom and spiritual force that we find in them now. As occultists, we are able to understand the communications relating to him, and we may even take them literally. For example, it is true when we read about him: "At his birth he shone like the bright light of the sun." We can also take it literally when Buddha says: "I have entered my last incarnation and need not return to earth unless I do it on my own free will." During the post-Atlantean epoch he also toiled to pass through stages of intellectual insights, and we can understand him when he says that the lines of incarnations and different stages of initiations through which he had passed flashed up before him:

Before me stood the splendor of the forms,
But my intuition was not yet pure!

I saw the Spirits of Insight,
But my intuition was not yet pure!

I saw the site of initiation,
But my intuition was not yet pure!

I was the companion among them:
Now my intuition was pure!

This is Buddha's illumination. He was one of those with whom we live in Rosicrucian theosophy.

We have already named three of the Masters: Zarathas, Skythianos, and Boddha or Buddha, and we can see how the lives of these leading personalities extend into our present time. An occultist can test these findings. In the realm of spiritual economy we not only find what these exalted men left behind; everything else that is of value to humanity is preserved. Take, for example, an individual such as Galileo, who in the sixteenth century achieved such significant results in physics. Galileo had an etheric body that was not allowed to die with him. Far away from the place where Galileo had worked, there lived a man in the middle of the eighteenth century who prepared himself for a great task after two decades of a devotional childhood. Deep in Russia, at the White Sea, lived a man in the plainest circumstances. His name was Michael Lomonosov. Unknown and without means, he hiked to Moscow and subsequently laid the foundations for Russian grammar. Lomonosov bore within him the etheric body of Galileo. And now it happened that a personality, who knew that the etheric body of Galileo had been preserved and who, in fact, had been present when this connection was being investigated occultly, knew nothing about Michael Lomonosov. This is no disgrace since on the physical plane one cannot know everything. But here we see that valuable elements are preserved and the past is connected with the future through the law of spiritual economy. In the Rosicrucian mysteries, too, we encounter the individuality who lived in the body of Buddha on the physical plane. During the Atlantean age, he had lived only as a bodhisattva, but later on he descended into the physical body of Buddha.

Let us now look at the times of Buddha and Zarathustra and observe what souls had to do in the ages between these two spiritual leaders. On the one hand, we have the teachings of Ahura Mazdao, on the other, that side of humanity that increasingly became fond of the earth. Let us envision once again the Indian, Persian, and Chaldean-Assyrian-Babylonian times during which the soul gradually lost its connection with the spiritual world. Then, in ancient Greece the soul came to love the earth so deeply that the statement of a famous Greek, "Better to be a beggar in the upper world than a king in the world of shadows," was accepted as truth. During this fourth post-Atlantean, the Graeco-Roman epoch, everything in the external world appeared to be beautiful and charming. The seer may, for example, observe the ruins of the Temple of Paestrum with his physical eye and revel admiringly in the beauty of the temple's form and in the intriguing charm of its lines. However, when he takes his eyes off the temple and looks for a similar substance in the spiritual world, he finds nothing. Everything seems to be blotted out. This is what these souls experienced between death and rebirth. They were isolated within the cold circumference of their individuality, cut off from all spiritual things and longing only for the physical world and all its beauty.

Ahura Mazdao himself, the Leader of the Sun, had to

descend to earth to bring light into this icy separateness. He had to become a human being in the physical world in order to help both the living and the dead. He had to be a human among humans! The high and the magnificent that lives in the sun descended to earth and revealed itself in and to humanity. Previously, it had revealed itself in the elements, for example to Moses in the fire of the burning bush and in the lightning on Sinai. The Israelites were to make no graven image of their God. Why? Because no external name can be given to "Me," the Divine Being; only an entirely different name can express the *"I am the I am!"* The only possibility of discovering the spirit of the sun's name is to seek it in the human being. That which lives as "I" in human beings is the Christ-Being.

The Jehova revelation precedes the Christ. That was at the time when the Christ-Being could gradually descend to the earth. What had Zarathustra once vowed to the high Sun-Being? What sacrifice did he want to make to him? His body, senses, life, and speech. Zarathustra was reincarnated as a contemporary of the great Buddha. He could then build up the etheric and astral bodies that he had sacrificed. He was reborn as Zarathas or Nazarathos, and he became the teacher of Pythagoras, who himself was reincarnated as one of the three Wise Men of the East and became one of the disciples of Jesus of Nazareth. Zarathustra, who had once sacrificed his etheric and astral bodies, was also able to give up his external sheath to Him whose coming he had once announced. As the Jesus of Nazareth of Western occultism, he could place his physical body at the disposal of the Sun Spirit and was then able to say, "I am the Light of the World!"

The Christ-Being was known in all the mysteries. In ancient India, at the time of the Seven Rishis, the being who represented Christ was called Vishva Karman. Zarathustra named him Ahura Mazdao, and in Egypt he was known as

153

Osiris. The Jewish people called him Jahve or Jehova, and then in the fourth cultural epoch this very same being lived for three years on our physical earth. This is the being who will in the future reunite the sun with the earth. Mystically, the Christ united Himself with the earth when the blood streamed from His wounds at Golgotha. At that time He appears in the aura of the earth, and He has been in it ever since.

Who was the first man to see Christ in the aura of the earth? It was St. Paul, who did more than anyone else for the dissemination of Christianity. What caused Saul to become Paul? Neither the teachings nor the events that took place in Palestine, but the event at Damascus, which was of a supersensible nature. Before that experience, Paul could not believe that the one who had died so disgracefully on the cross had been the Christ, but as an initiate of the cabala he knew that the Christ would be visible in the aura of the earth once He had appeared on earth. That was the experience of Paul, which transformed him from Saul to Paul. Paul said of himself that he was born prematurely, and the same is also said of the Buddha. This means that such an individuality does not descend too deeply into the physical realm. When Paul became clairvoyant before he came to Damascus, he saw and knew who Christ was.

The Christ was working in Buddha as a bodhisattva, and it was He who was now the planetary spirit of the earth since the event of Golgotha and who could since be found in the physical aura of the earth. Through the Christ-Principle a new light has been kindled in this world and beyond. The body of Jesus of Nazareth—the etheric and astral bodies and the ego of Jesus of Nazareth—exist in many copies in the spiritual world. Such a statement expresses something of great significance, and for a better understanding of it we can draw on nature for a number of enlightening examples. Just think of a grain seed that grows into a stalk and multiplies itself many times in the process. This apparently simple natural process is a parable of the events in the supersensible world that are governed by certain laws. Many copies of the etheric and astral bodies and of the ego of Jesus of Nazareth exist in order to be incorporated in the preliminary bearers of the Christ-Principle. Everything connected with the Christ-Principle is so momentous that humanity can grasp it only little by little.

St. Augustine, for example, bore within him a copy of the etheric body of Jesus of Nazareth; and once you know that, you will be able to appreciate his life, his errors, and his accomplishments. His ego and his astral body were left to their own resources, and only in his etheric body did his great mystical gift come to life. St. Francis of Assisi and Thomas Aquinas had copies of the astral body of Jesus of Nazareth woven into their souls, and it is this fact that allowed them to be such dynamic teachers. They worked from a sphere in which Christ had once lived.

In some cases external events such as natural catastrophes or similar things enhance this weaving of spiritual bodies into the soul of the recipient. It is said of St. Thomas Aquinas that lightning struck and killed his little sister in the room where he happened to be standing, but spared him. He interpreted this lightning bolt next to him to the effect that elemental forces were necessary to help him take up the copy of the astral body of Jesus of Nazareth. Elisabeth of Thüringen also had an imprint of the astral body of Jesus of Nazareth in her soul.

Zarathustra, or Jesus of Nazareth, is one of the three Masters of the Rosicrucians. Many copies of his ego, that is of the ego in which the Christ Spirit Himself had dwelled, can be found in the spiritual world. The copies of the ego of Jesus of Nazareth are waiting for us in the spiritual world to be utilized for the future evolution of humankind. People who endeavor to strive upward to the heights of spiritual wisdom and love are candidates for these copies of the ego of Jesus of Nazareth. They become bearers of Christ, true Christophori. On this earth they shall be heralds of His Second Coming.

We derive strength for our future work from the knowledge of which individualities are behind the missions of important human beings. It is possible to test these facts. Not everyone is able to investigate what goes on behind the curtains of the physical world, but everyone can examine the results of such investigations by looking at the Holy Scriptures written before and after Christ. These facts can illuminate the way to understanding; and if they do, they change within us and become spiritual life blood.

Footnotes

[1]The "original" Zarathustra (or Zoroaster) Rudolf Steiner refers to in these lectures is not the historical religious teacher and prophet of ancient Persia whose dates are ca. 628 B.C.-551 B.C., but the prophet who, according to early Christian tradition and according to Plutarch was born about 6400 B.C. He gave the impulse for the founding of the second post-Atlantean epoch.

[2]The term *maya* in the Hindu Veda means magic power, but in Mahayana Buddhism it denotes illusion or non-reality; and this is how Steiner uses the term.

[3]Historical scholarship usually considers Hermes as a mythical figure in ancient Egypt, but Steiner thinks he was a living prophet who appeared about 4200 B.C. when the sun moved into Taurus. According to historical speculation the so-called Hermetic books—metaphysical pronouncements about the community of all beings and things—were authored by the Egyptian god Thoth (the Thrice Great), whose name was often translated into Greek as Hermes Trismegistus.

[4]The "Akasha Chronicle" is an occult "script" containing the complete story of the universe. Occultists of all ages have tried to "read" it by freeing themselves from the limitations of time and space. Rudolf Steiner had refined his spiritual faculties to such a degree that he was able to read the "Akasha Chronicle." To understand his work, it is necessary to assume that he did possess this capacity. For a thorough description of the nature of the Akasha Chronicle, see Rudolf Steiner, *Cosmic Memory*, pp. 38-41.

[5]Nicholas of Cusa (1401?-1464) was a German humanist, scientist, and philosopher of the highest rank who became Bishop of Brixon in 1450. His astounding achievements in science included a theory that the Earth revolves on its axis around the sun and that the stars are different worlds.

[6]Polish-born Nicholas Copernicus (1473-1543) was the founder of modern astronomy. His main work on the orbits and revolutions of heavenly bodies, completed in 1530, but not published until 1543 when he was on his deathbed, expressed his views on the structure of the physical universe.

157

⁷Galileo Galilei (1564-1642) was the great Italian astronomer, mathematician, and physicist who laid the foundations of modern experimental science. The time of his death in the text (toward the end of the seventeenth century) is an error in transcription.

⁸Gottfried Wilhelm von Leibniz (1646-1716) was the famous German philosopher, mathematician, and statesman who invented calculus independent from Newton and is widely regarded as the founder of symbolic logic. His philosophical achievements include the *Theodicy* and the famous *Monadology*.

⁹Sir Isaac Newton (1642-1727) was the great English mathematician and physicist whose works marked a turning point in modern experimental science. Few people know that in the later years of his life Newton spent much of his time in the study of theology and alchemy.

¹⁰Michail Vasilyevich Lomonosov (1712-65) was perhaps the most outstanding scientist, scholar, and writer of eighteenth-century Russia.

¹¹Pythagoras (c. 582-c. 507 B.C.) was a pre-Socratic Greek philosopher and mathematician of whose personal life traditional science knows little. He migrated from his native Samos to Gotona and established a mystery center. The followers of Pythagoras believed, among other things, in the transmigration of souls.

¹²Melchizedek was the king of Salem and "Priest of the Most High God," who blessed Abraham after the defeat of Chedorlaomer (Genesis 14:18-20) and who was later to typify the priesthood of the future Messiah (Psalms 110:4; Heb. 5-7).

¹³St. Irenaeus (c. 125-c. 202) was a Greek theologian, Bishop of Lyons in 177-78, and the first Father of the Catholic Church to systematize Christian doctrine.

¹⁴Papias was a second-century Christian theologian and Apostolic Father of the Church.

¹⁵St. Augustine (354-430) was the Bishop of Hippo in what is now Algiers and one of the four Latin fathers. His famous book *The City of God* is a justification of Christianity against pagan critics, and his *Confessions* is a classic of Christian mysticism.

¹⁶*Heliand*, the title of the epic (c. 825) is an Old Saxon word for German *Heiland* = the Savior. The poem had 5,983 lines and was written in alliterative verse.

¹⁷The Italian St. Francis of Assisi (1182-1226) was one of the greatest Christian saints and founder of the Franciscan Order.

¹⁸Elisabeth of Thüringen (1207-1231), the young widow of a German margrave who had died on a crusade in 1227, chose a life of poverty, humility, and charity and became the typical saint of the late Middle Ages.

[19]Scholasticism was the school of thought in the Middle Ages in which theology and philosophy were conjoined. The German term *Scholastik* normally designates this medieval school of thought, whereas *Scholastizismus*, the linguistic equivalent of the English term, is used exclusively to denote sophistry and casuitry.

[20]Meister (Johannes) Eckhart (c. 1260-1328), a Dominican-trained German theologian and the most profound of the German medieval mystics, was probably the first writer of speculative prose in German.

[21]Johannes Tauler (1300-1361) was a German Dominican mystic and a disciple of Meister Eckhart.

[22]The Hussites advocated communion in both kinds, i.e., both wine and bread, for laity as well as priests. Lutherans believed that a change takes place by which the body and blood of Christ join with the bread and wine. This principle of consubstantiation was rejected by the Zwinglians who saw only symbolic significance in the communion. Finally, the Calvinists believed that Christ was spiritually, but not physically, present in the Sacrament.

[23]Giordano Bruno (1548-1600) was a noted Italian philosopher and mystic who, although a member of the Dominican Order in his youth, was in constant opposition to religious orthodox schools. He was tried by the Inquisition for heresy and burned to death.

[24]Ernst Haeckel (1834-1932) was a renowned German zoologist and, like the English naturalist Charles Robert Darwin (1809-1882), developed a theory of evolution. Emil DuBois-Reymond (1818-1896) was a famous physiologist in Berlin. Thomas Henry Huxley (1825-1895) was an English biologist and writer.

[25]David Friedrich Strauss (1808-1874) was a philosopher and theologian whose writings mark a turning point in the critical study of the life of Jesus. In his main work, *The Life of Jesus* (2 vols, 1835-36), Strauss applied the "myth theory" to the life of Jesus and denied all supernatural elements in the Gospels.

[26](Old) Saturn, (Old) Sun, and (Old) Moon are names for *former* evolutionary forms through which the Earth has passed. The reader is referred to Chapter 4 of Rudolf Steiner, *An Outline of Occult Science* (Anthroposophic Press, 1972), for a thorough discussion of this topic.

[27]The Vedas are the oldest scriptures of Hinduism. The Veda is the literature of the Aryans who invaded NW India about 1500 B.C. and pertains to the fire sacrifice central to their religious beliefs.

[28]The Upanishads constitute the last section of the Hindu Veda and are said to have been composed around 900 B.C. As the wellspring of Hindu speculative and religious thought, they became the basis for the later

159

schools of Vedanta. "Vedanta" literally means "The end of the Veda" and refers to how the Upanishads are to be taught and interpreted.

[29] John Scotus Erigena (c. 810–c. 877) was an Irish scholastic philosopher.

[30] St. Thomas Aquinas (1225–1274) was the Italian theologian and philosopher whose philosophy was declared the official philosophy of the Catholic Church. He is generally regarded to have been the most prominent mind of scholasticism.

[31] Christian Rosenkreutz is generally regarded by most scholars as the pseudonym for the German writer Johan Valentin Andrea (1586–1654). In his works *Fama fraternitatis* (1614) and in *Confessio rosae crucis* (1615), he traced the development of the Rosicrucian Society to Arab and Oriental origins.

[32] The German noun forms *Atem* and *Atmung* mean breath and breathing, respectively, whereas the verb for "to breathe" is *atmen*.

[33] The works of the Greek philosopher Aristotle (384–322 B.C.) became the basis of medieval scholasticism and had a decisive influence on Catholic theology.

[34] Dionysius the Aeropagite is said to have been the first Bishop of Athens, Greece, in the first century A.C. Tradition has made him a martyr and Acts 17:34 tells of his conversion by Paul.

[35] Johann Wolfgang von Goethe (1749–1832) was Germany's greatest poet. Early in his academic career, Steiner spent several years editing Goethe's scientific writings, and during his lifetime he did not tire of extolling Goethean perception and thinking. The main seat of the Anthroposophic movement in Dornach, Switzerland, is still called the "Goetheanum." Steiner gave several lecture cycles on Goethe's great poem *Faust*. These have been published as *Faust, der strebende Mensch*, Vol. I, and *Geisteswissenschaftliche Erläuterungen zu Goethe's "Faust"* Vol. II (Rudolf Steiner Verlag: Dornach, 1974).

[36] Exodus 3:14.

[37] The *Bhagavad Gita* is a religious Hindu poem consisting of dialogues between Prince Arjuna and Krishna, who reveals himself as the *avatara* (incarnation) of Vishnu. The transcription of the quotation from the *"Gita"* is probably a contraction of several textual citations on pp. 452, 522, and 529, among others, of *Bhagavad-gita AS IT IS*. Complete edition (Collier Books: New York, 1974).

[38] Goethe, *Faust* II, lines 12104–12111:

CHORUS MYSTCUS
> What is destructible
> Is but a parable;
> What fails ineluctably,

160

The undeclarable,
Here it was seen,
Here it was action;
The Eternal-Feminine
Lures to perfection.
(Translation by Walter Kaufmann)

These are the very last lines of Goethe's *Faust*, indicating that the things of this material world are but a symbolic expression of the spiritual world. Love, through its embodiment in women, remains the guiding force for the striving human being.

[39]Faust has been blinded by Care (*Sorge*), an allegorical figure, and exclaims:

Deep night now seems to fall more deeply still,
Yet inside me there shines a brilliant light;
What I have thought, I hasten to fulfill:
The master's word alone has real might.
(Faust II, lines 11499-11502. Trsl. by Walter Kaufmann)

[40]Columban (545-615) was an Irish missionary.

[41]Gallus was a sixth-century Irish-Scotch missionary.

[42]Patrick (c. 384-c. 460) was an English missionary.

[43]Steiner is referring to the German courtly epic *Parzival* by Wolfram von Eschenbach (about 1200/10). The Frenchman Chrétien de Troyes was the author of the first great artistic treatment of the theme; in his unfinished poem "Percivale" finds the Grail and heals the king. Wolfram's story is drawn from Chrétien's model but is much more spiritualized in its triadic structure: innocence, fall, salvation. The Simpleton Parsifal is educated as a knight who knows proper courtly behavioral codes, one of them being not to ask too many questions. This attitude causes him to be expelled from the Grail's Castle, and only after he has undergone a second, Christian phase of education does he know how to express his charity by asking the appropriate question of the ailing king.

[44]Homer, *Odyssey*, Canto 489-491. These words are spoken by the soul of Achilles after Ulysses had conjured it up from the Underworld.

161

A Note on the Transcription of Lectures

From Rudolf Steiner's Autobiography
The Course of My Life, **XXXV** (1925)

My anthroposophical work has yielded two results: first, the books I have published for all the world to read; secondly, a number of lecture courses which were at first intended for private printing and were to be for sale only to members of the Theosophical (later the Anthroposophical) Society. These were reports of my lecture, more or less accurate, which I did not have the time to correct. I would have preferred oral pronouncements to have remained just that, but the members wanted a private printing of these courses and that is what was done. Had I had the time to correct the transcriptions, the restriction "for members only" would have been unnecessary from the very beginning. Now, for more than a year, the restriction has been omitted anyway.

Here, in *The Course of My Life*, it is above all necessary to state how the published books and the privately printed material combine into what I developed as anthroposophy.

Whoever wants to trace my inner struggles and see how I worked to acquaint contemporary consciousness with anthroposophy must do so on the basis of publications that were intended for the general public. It is in them that I dealt with everything that in our time qualifies as the search for knowledge. The reader will find in these works what increasingly took form within me through "spiritual perception" and what became—albeit incompletely in many ways —the edifice of anthroposophy.

One requirement that emerged was to build "anthroposophy" and thereby respond to the need of imparting information from the spiritual world to the generally educated public of our time. Soon, however, it also became necessary to fully address what from within the membership revealed itself as spiritual needs and intellectual longings.

Above all, a strong inclination was felt to have the Gospels and the Bible presented in the light of what had emerged as anthroposophical inquiry. The members in the courses wanted to hear about the revelations that mankind had been given.

In response to this request, internal lecture courses were given which were attended only by members. They, however, were familiar with the rudimentary pronouncements about anthroposophy so that one could speak to them as one would to advanced students of anthroposophy. The approach in these internal lectures was different from the one necessary for the publications that were entirely intended for the general public.

In these inner circles it was appropriate for me to discuss the subject matter in a less structured way. If the same subject matter had from the outset been designated for public presentation, I would have had no choice but to rearrange things accordingly.

Thus, something is indeed present in the two endeavors, in public and private writings, which derives from two different backgrounds. The exclusively public writings are the result of what struggled and was at work in me, whereas in the privately printed material the society joins me in my struggle and labor. When it does, I listen to the pulsations in the soul-life of the members and as I vividly partake in what they have to say, the lecture takes shape.

At no time is anything whatsoever mentioned in the lectures that is not the clearest result of the developing anthroposophy and absolutely no concession is made to accommodate the members' prejudices or preconceived notions. Anyone reading this privately printed material can accept its contents in the fullest sense as a pronouncement of what anthroposophy has to say. Therefore, when complaints in this regard became too persistent, we could without hesitation abandon the practice of distributing the printed material only to members. What will have to be accepted, however, is that the transcriptions not checked by me may contain some errors.

We will concede the right of judging the content of this printed material only to those who know what is acceptable as a prerequisite for making such a judgment. The *minimal* prerequisite for an appreciation of this printed material is that one has an anthroposophical understanding of man, and of the cosmos to the extent that its nature is explained by anthroposophy. Moreover, one should know "anthroposophical history" as manifested in the pronouncements from the spiritual world.

CPSIA information can be obtained
at www.ICGtesting.com
Printed in the USA
FSHW011912130319
56338FS